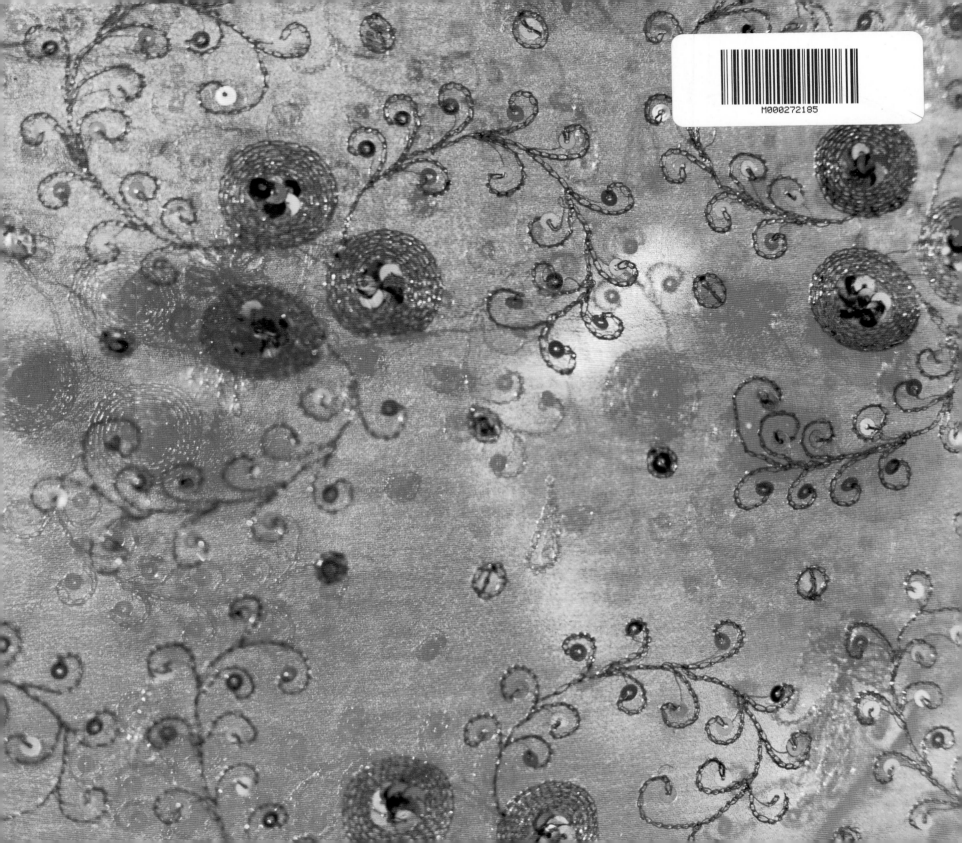

Approach cooking, and love, with audacity.

CAROLINE HOFBERG

MOROCCO

on a Plate

Breads, Entrees, and Desserts with Authentic Spice

Translated by
Paulina Björk Kapsalis

SKYHORSE PUBLISHING

Skyhorse Publishing books may be purchased in bulk at special discounts for sales promotion, corporate gifts, fund-raising, or educational purposes. Special editions can also be created to specifications. For details, contact the Special Sales Department, Skyhorse Publishing, 307 West 36th Street, 11th Floor, New York, NY 10018 or info@skyhorsepublishing.com.

Skyhorse® and Skyhorse Publishing® are registered trademarks of Skyhorse Publishing, Inc.®, a Delaware corporation.

www.skyhorsepublishing.com

10 9 8 7 6 5 4 3 2 1

Library of Congress Cataloging-in-Publication Data is available on file.

Print ISBN: 978-1-62914-414-6
Ebook ISBN: 978-1-63220-054-9

Cover design by Rain Saukas

Printed in China

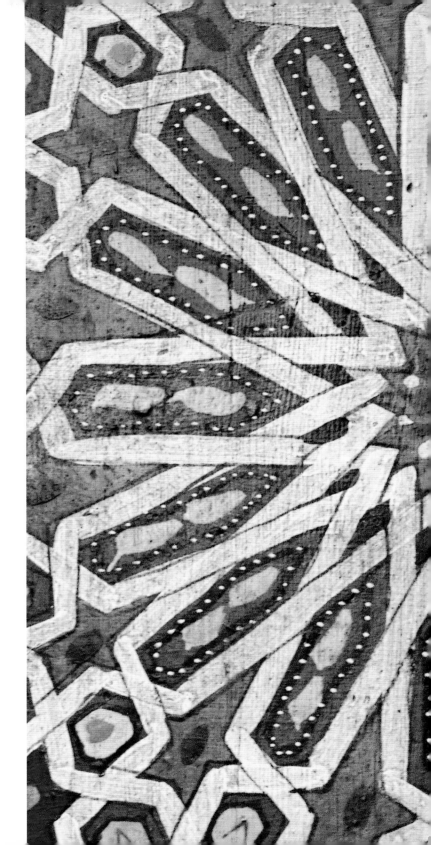

CONTENTS

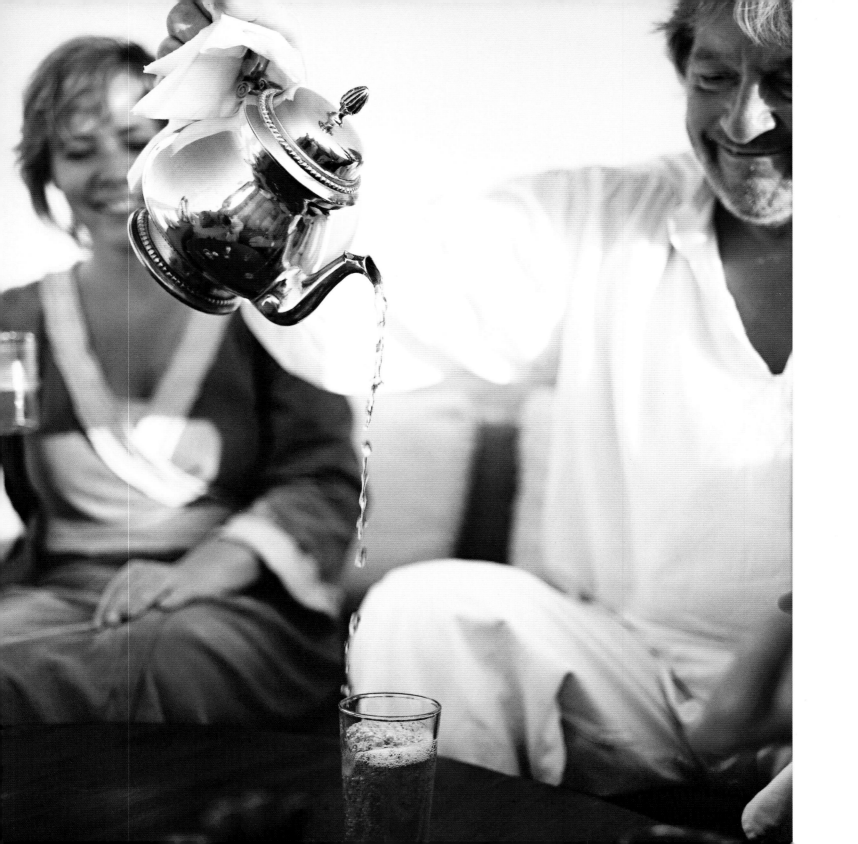

PREFACE

We leave on a day in September. We're a diverse group of people meeting at Arlanda Airport. There is my wonderful photographer, Tina, with her family: Boris, a three-month-old with a brand new passport, proud big sister Olga, and daddy Oskar. And then there is my patient husband, Ove, who is also the graphic designer of this book, and our good friend Peter, an interior designer with lots of knowledge about Morocco (thank you Peter for sharing your contacts).

The more adventurous and less conventional, the better. That seems to be our motto. When we are given the choice, we pick camping stoves, simple environments, and heavy lifting over fancy photo studios, delicate porcelain, and trendy food. On this trip, there will be a few challenges, but also a lot of laughter. It's not the most organized trip we've made, but that makes it all the more charming and enjoyable.

Our first day of adventures is finally upon us. There is a knock on my door. But not literally because there are no doors here. Tina peeks at me from behind a curtain, whispering to see if I'm up. I'm already awake, obviously. We're staying in the oldest part of Marrakech, right next to a mosque, and the muezzin starts his day by calling the city to prayer before sunrise. We're headed out to watch the city wake up for the workday before it gets too hot. It's easy to get lost when you're new to the city and not fully awake, but fortunately for us, strangers help us find our way.

This is how we spend our days in Morocco: we wake up early each morning, explore the city, and then we start the cooking. Working in an environment filled with kind and helpful people and amazing ingredients is an invigorating way to jumpstart imagination and creativity, and a perfect delight for our taste buds. The evenings are filled with pleasant activities, such as visits to the marketplace at Jemaa el-Fnaa square. At dusk the barbecues are lit, tables and benches are put out, and the whole square is transformed into a meeting place where everything centers around food. For a small fee, you can try all sorts of wonderful dishes and be surrounded by street life, barbecue smoke, and the buzz of people socializing. Behind the square hides a labyrinth of little alleys that make up the street market. It is often packed with people, donkeys, mopeds, and stray cats. Visitors purchase spices, leather, brass, silver, fabrics, ceramics, mosaics, rugs, and slippers. With everything in one delightful area, it's no coincidence that chefs, decorators, and designers are all turning their attention to Morocco for inspiration. Moroccan culture truly makes an impression on everyone.

The fragrances, the flavors, the colors. The stands selling olives, pickled lemons, and pastries. The spices arranged beautifully like art. All of this creates an inspiring image. Of course I fall in love with it all! In Sweden, where I'm from, we are used to spices packed tightly into sterile, fragrance-blocking glass or plastic containers. We barely know what a vanilla bean or a cinnamon stick look like. The pepper is preground and the salt has a brand name. To us Swedes, spices like saffron, cinnamon, cloves, and cardamom are associated with pastries and Christmas. Dried fruits are also strictly a Christmas treat to us northerners. Little boxes of dates and figs are arranged on platters with mixed nuts, to gather dust all through the holidays. In Morocco, the spices are put to use in different ways, and that inspires me.

This book is an expression of my love for Moroccan food. I've taken all my favorites, explored and experimented with them to create what is finally Morocco—my way. So come along and join me on a truly exciting food journey!

Caroline Hofberg

In Morocco, the kitchen is the women's domain. Most women still spend all their time in the home, and lots of it cooking. There is a sense of affinity here—the women talk, laugh, and tell stories.

MOROCCAN CUISINE

THE FLAVORS, THE FRAGRANCES, THE COLORS

The roots of Moroccan cuisine lie in the simple food of the nomads. It's been altered by adding spices, and influenced by the fingerprint of all the different cultures that have passed through the region. It is an exciting mix of African, Oriental, and European influences. The ancient Mediterranean cultures, the nomads, the Turks, and the French all left their imprint.

It is a colorful cuisine that breathes romance and brings to mind the tales of the *Arabian Nights*. You can practically taste the mysticism of Arabian culture. It's a treat for all senses and a paradise for the food lover. Let yourself get swept away by the piquant smells of an exotic world. First and foremost, it is the spices, the dried fruit, the almonds, beans, lentils, couscous, and the olives that stand out and give Moroccan cuisine its charm.

A new food experience waits at every corner; just follow your nose and you'll find your way. The many fragrances at the bazaar spread through the streets. The spice stands with their beautifully displayed spices in vivid colors: Saffron, cinnamon, cloves, cumin. . . . Can you smell them?

The men rarely enter the kitchen, but they know exactly how the food should taste. They also know how to find the best vegetables at the market, as they're the ones who do the grocery shopping. Outside of the big cities, women are rarely seen out on the street.

HISTORICAL FOOD

Many Moroccan dishes are nothing short of history on a plate. The Arabs left the most obvious imprint on Mediterranean cuisines. From sometime during the seventh century until the gradual fall of the kingdom in the twelfth century, the Arabs ruled the Mediterranean area.

The Arabs brought many new ingredients and ideas. They colonized new areas, and traveled the world as merchants and missionaries. Their caravans made long and arduous journeys all the way to the Far East, where they picked up silk, spices, and knowledge. The marketplace in Constantinople (Istanbul) was, for hundreds of years, the largest market for spices. Today, people in North Africa still use many of the spices brought to Morocco by the Arabs in the seventh century. The Arabs also brought new fruits and vegetables from the Far East: eggplants, citrus fruits, and peaches. It became customary to give fruit or almond trees away as presents.

The Persians also played an important part in shaping the Mediterranean cuisines. Persian cuisine was considered very elegant. They used fruit in dishes with meat and poultry to create a balance between sweet and sour. This symbolized the fight between good and evil. The tradition of cooking this way has been traced all the way back to the third century. The contrast between sweet and sour is still prominent in Moroccan food today, and dried fruit is still commonly used, especially in stews with lamb or chicken. In this way, history is present every time you sit down to eat. In this book you will find many recipes for full-bodied stews, with an intriguing contrast of flavors created by adding dried fruit.

Creativity is important, and the women have a wonderful imagination when it comes to using their ingredients in new ways. The girls grow up in the kitchen, and their mothers teach them how to cook from a young age.

THE MAGIC OF SPICES

Morocco, in northern Africa, isn't that far from Spain and France in southern Europe. Only the Mediterranean Sea separates them. While traveling through these countries, you can clearly see how food traditions have crossed cultural borders throughout history. Merchants, crusaders, and wars all altered the food in some way, and it can be hard to know where some dishes originated.

Over two thousand years ago, Morocco, Tunisia, Algeria, and Libya were one country: Magreb. It was populated by nomads, now known as the Berbers. There are still millions of people with Berber lineage living in North Africa.

The old Magreb is the reason that North African cuisines are so similar. Couscous is the staple food of the whole area. The concept of mixing meat with dried fruit, the various types of stews, and sweet pastries all remain mostly the same in the countries that were once part of Magreb. What separates the food in these countries is mostly the spice. Moroccan cuisine is considered the greatest and most refined, with its mild and full-bodied flavors.

Throughout history, many kings and emperors have ruled Morocco. While Europe was still suffering through the dark middle ages, the royal courts of Morocco enjoyed luxurious lives and a booming cultural scene. Spices and power went hand in hand; using lots of spices was a way to exhibit wealth.

Little did they know back then that the magic of spices would later entrance the rest of the world as well. Trendsetting chefs from all over the globe are now being inspired by Moroccan cuisine, and strive to present the *Arabian Nights* on a plate. They aim to copy its colors, and the exuberance and the dreams it represents.

COMMON INGREDIENTS

ORANGE FLOWER WATER The word *alcohol* is Arabic (*al'khahal*), and we use it because it was the Arabs who discovered the art of distillation. Orange flower water (or orange blossom water) is produced from orange blossoms, which are harvested every spring. They are left to dry on large pieces of cloth for two days, and then distilled. The aromatic essence is used in salads, pastries, and desserts. Orange flower water can be found in well-stocked supermarkets and liquor stores, or in Middle Eastern grocery stores. In some cases it can also be replaced with orange zest.

ROSE WATER Every spice stand in Morocco sells dried rosebuds. They are used in different spice blends and in rose water, which is used in perfumes but also in pastries. It is also common to splash your hands in rose water after a meal. Dried rose petals are also frequently used to add a flowery touch to mint tea. You can buy rose water where you find orange blossom water. Look in the ethnic food section and in the baking aisle. The flavor of rose water is unique, and cannot be substituted.

CHERMOULA Chermoula is a thick sauce made from herbs, spices, garlic, olive oil, and lemon juice. It can be used as a marinade, as stuffing for fish, or as a side dish. The recipes vary slightly. (p. 25)

RAS EL HANOUT Ras el hanout is Morocco's most famous spice blend. It consists of at least ten, but often up to thirty, different kinds of spices, such as cinnamon, cumin, cloves, turmeric, black pepper, and rosebuds. Every salesman has his own blend, with his own secret recipe. The Moroccan housewife usually begins cooking by mixing up this blend. It is worthwhile to make your own. (p. 23)

HARISSA Harissa is a spice blend made from chili peppers. It is common both as a dried spice mix, and as a thick paste. Originally a Tunisian blend, it is now popular everywhere in North Africa. You can find it in well-stocked supermarkets and Middle Eastern grocery stores, or you can make your own. (p. 27)

SAFFRON The king of spices. Saffron is made from the stamens of a flower commonly known as the saffron crocus. In Morocco, it is grown in the fertile valley of Souss, which lies south of Agadir. Around 75,000 flowers are needed to make a pound of dry saffron. It is one of the spices brought to the Mediterranean area from the Middle East long before our time. The Moors were the ones to start growing the crocus flowers closer to home, in Spain, during the eighth century. When they were forced out of Spain in the fifteenth century, they brought their knowledge with them to Morocco. Saffron became an important ingredient in the refined cuisine of the Moroccan royal court. It was worth its weight in gold, and selling fake saffron was a very serious crime. Forgery still takes place today, as saffron is still the most expensive spice in the world.

FRESH HERBS Cilantro, parsley, and mint are the most common herbs used in Moroccan cooking. Fresh cilantro, with its distinct flavor, and its dried seeds (coriander seeds) are both used in Moroccan cuisine. Mint is without a doubt the most common herb in Morocco, but it's not used much in the food. It's used more for making mint tea (recipe on p. 72). The mint is purchased daily from the street market, where you will find fresh leaves in huge piles on the sidewalk. Every day you'll see men on their way home from work, with a bunch of mint tucked under their arm (photo on pp. 70–71).

DRIED SPICES Cumin, coriander, ginger, paprika, cinnamon, chili, turmeric, and saffron are the most common dried spices. They are combined in different ways and in different proportions. Cumin is an important spice—and an important fragrance—in Moroccan cuisine. It is often mixed with salt and served as a table condiment. To get the best flavor, toast the seeds in a hot pan before grinding them. Anise seeds are also common, especially when baking. Cinnamon is used a lot, grinded or not, in stews, vegetable dishes, and desserts. Ground cinnamon is also used to decorate food, such as pastille (photo on p. 98).

BROAD BEANS Broad beans are green, flat pods, each containing two to seven seeds. You only eat the seeds. The flavor is fresh but strong, and they are great in soups and salads. Originally, broad beans were grown only in the Mediterranean, but now you can find them anywhere. Your best chance of finding fresh broad beans is in the summer. (Photo and recipes on pp. 43, 47, & 67.)

OKRA The plant is three to seven feet tall, and self-fertilizing. The green fruit, which is often referred to as ladies' fingers, is three inches long and sometimes hairy. The fruit is harvested before ripening and used in soups or fried. When cooked, okra exudes a sticky juice that thickens the soup or sauce. (Photo and recipe on pp. 37 & 81.)

BREAD Bread is considered Allah's most precious gift, and is treated with much respect. Beggars in the streets can often be heard saying, "Give me bread in the name of Allah." Bread is treated with reverence; much like rice is in Asia, and to the Berbers, bread dipped in oil is a sacred meal. If you drop a piece of bread on the floor, you pick it up and kiss it. Bread is a staple food and the base of every meal. Tradition calls for the host to break the bread and hand a piece to every guest.

TAJINE (TAGINE) A tajine is a clay pot that has a cone-shaped lid and a hole at the top, which lets the steam escape. It is also the name of the dish that is cooked in the pot, often a stew with meat, chicken, fish, or vegetables. When the stew is ready, it is served over hot couscous. You will find recipes for many rich stews in this book. If you can't find a tajine, use your regular stew pot. (Photos on pp. 91 & 100.)

COUSCOUS Couscous was originally created out of necessity, as a way to preserve wheat. The tiny hard grains are made from durum wheat dough, which is pressed through fine sieves. The grains are then left to dry in the sun. Couscous is served as a main dish with an assortment of condiments at special occasions when the whole family is together. In Morocco, this usually happens on Fridays, the Muslim day of prayer. It is cooked in a special steamer pot, where a stew cooks in the bottom piece, and a couscous steamer fits on top. Most of the couscous sold in our supermarkets has been precooked, so all you have to do is add boiling water and wait a few minutes. (Recipe on p. 59.)

DATES The Arabs believe that when God created Earth, he made the date palm from what was left after creating Adam. Dates, camel meat, and milk were the most common foods of the nomads. During Ramadan—the month of fasting—the fast is broken with dates every evening. They are also enjoyed as snacks and used in baking and desserts. Dried dates are often found in stews with meat or chicken. There are more than twenty different kinds of dates.

ALMONDS In the summer, when it's almond season, the almonds are eaten fresh. They are then dried and used in desserts, pastries, and savory dishes all year-round. It is an ingredient you can always find in large amounts in every Moroccan home.

OLIVES Olives are served with every meal in North Africa, and are an integral part of the culture. There are many different varieties. At the souks (marketplaces) you will find a multitude of olives of varying size, consistency and color. Each type will have its own unique flavor and character. The green olives are immature and the black ones are mature. (Photos on pp. 29 & 65.)

PRESERVED LEMONS A Moroccan classic. You can find a large jar of preserved lemons in every Moroccan home, where they are used to add a distinct tangy flavor to stews and salads. Sometimes the salted lemons are soaked in olive oil, which makes them keep longer, and gives them a more full-bodied, milder flavor. If you can't find them at your supermarket (check the olive bar) or at a Middle Eastern market, you can make your own. (Recipe on p. 68 and photos on pp. 29 & 65.)

GREEN TEA Green tea came to Morocco from China or Japan during the Crimean War in the nineteenth century, when the English tradesmen could no longer sell it to Eastern Europe. Large quantities were sold to North Africa, where it quickly became very popular. The people of Morocco made it their own by adding the spices they loved and were accustomed to—mint in particular. (Recipe on p. 72.)

SPICE BLENDS

RAS EL HANOUT

This is Morocco's most famous spice blend, and can contain up to thirty different spices. It's a popular ingredient during the winter, as it adds heat to stews and cous-cous dishes. Each salesman has his own secret recipe. Sometimes the blend contains dried rosebuds, and the salesman will tell you about the great effect it will have on your love life. Read more about ras el hanout on p. 17.

3 cardamom pods
1 cinnamon stick
5 bay leaves
1 tbsp dried thyme
1 tbsp black peppercorns
1 tbsp cloves
1 tbsp coriander seeds
1 tsp mace
½ tsp ground ginger
1 tsp cumin seeds
1 tsp turmeric
1 tsp anise seeds
1 tsp cayenne pepper
2 tbsp paprika

▨ Pick the cardamom seeds out of their pods and break the cinnamon stick into smaller pieces.

▨ Grind everything in an electric spice or coffee grinder, or use a mortar and pestle.

▨ Store the blend in a well-sealed jar.

CHERMOULA

There are many versions of this spice blend, which is more like a paste than a dry mix. You can use it for many things. I love to use it to marinate or gratinate meat, fish, or poultry. It is also great flavoring in stews and pasta dishes. Store the blend in the fridge. Read more about chermoula on p. 17, and see the recipe for Mediterranean Fish Stew on p. 128.

2 tsp cumin seeds
1 tsp paprika
1 tsp coarse salt
2 large garlic cloves
3 tbsp chopped cilantro
3 tbsp chopped fresh parsley
3 tbsp lemon juice
3 tbsp olive oil

Roast the cumin seeds in a dry pan.

Grind the cumin, salt, garlic, cilantro, and parsley with the paprika using a mortar and pestle, until it reaches a paste-like consistency.

Add lemon juice and olive oil and mix well.

HARISSA

Harissa is a chili paste from Tunisia that is now common in all of North Africa. It is used in stews and couscous dishes, and even as a table condiment so those who like their food spicy can season their meal to their preferred flavor. A great trick is to mix a little bit of harissa with a nice hot bouillon, which can then be drizzled over the food. It actually goes well with most food, in the right proportions. You can buy it at well-stocked supermarkets and Middle Eastern grocery stores. Read more about harissa on p. 17.

2⅔ oz (75 g) dried red chilies
3 garlic cloves, chopped
2 tsp coriander seeds
2 tsp cumin seeds
½ tsp coarse ground black pepper
½ tsp salt
3½ tbsp (50 ml) olive oil

▣ Soak the chilies in cold water for a few hours. Drain.

▣ Mix the chilies with garlic, coriander, cumin, salt, and pepper until it reaches a coarse paste-like consistency.

▣ Add the olive oil and mix well. Pour into a glass jar, drizzle a bit of olive oil on top, and close with a tight lid.

VEGETARIAN DISHES & SIDE DISHES

MOROCCAN ORANGE AND OLIVE SALAD

4 servings

4 oranges
1 small red onion
½ cup (100 ml) high-quality black olives
   with pits, such as Kalamata
¼ cup (50 ml) chopped parsley
2 tbsp sesame seeds

dressing
the juice from the oranges
2 tbsp olive oil
½ tsp ground cumin
salt and freshly ground pepper

Oranges and olives. A nice, fresh salad doesn't have to contain vegetables; the base can just as easily be fruit. Oranges are a winter fruit, which, in this salad, will add color and brighten your day.

▣ Peel the oranges with a knife, removing all the white pith. Cut them into slices across the membranes and arrange over a large plate. Save any juices from cutting the oranges for the dressing.

▣ Peel and slice the onions and separate into rings. Spread the onions, olives, and parsley over the oranges.

▣ Mix the ingredients for the dressing and drizzle it over the salad. Keep the salad cold in the fridge until it's time to serve.

▣ Roast the sesame seeds in a dry pan, and sprinkle over the salad before serving.

ORANGE SALAD WITH DATES

4 servings

4 oranges
½ cup (100 ml) shredded dates
lettuce, such as romaine and endive

dressing:
the juice from the oranges
2 tbsp olive oil
¼ tsp cinnamon
½ tsp ground cumin
¼–½ tsp harissa, store bought or homemade
   (p. 27)
salt

This salad is a must at Christmas. Oranges, dates, and cinnamon are all traditional Christmas flavors. I try to use two kinds of lettuce, preferably with a bit of bitterness to contrast the fruit's sweetness.

▣ Peel the oranges with a knife, removing all the white pith. Cut it into segments, and mix with dates in a bowl. Save the juices from cutting the oranges for the dressing.

▣ Mix the ingredients for the dressing and drizzle over the salad. Leave the salad to cool in the fridge for at least an hour. This will strengthen the flavor.

▣ Wash the lettuce and tear it apart. Use your hands to tear it, rather than a knife, to give the salad more volume.

▣ Serve on a large plate, with the orange salad on top of the lettuce. Pour the orange salad over the lettuce just before serving. This allows the lettuce to stay crisp.

GROUND LAMB CIGARS

8 pieces

4 phyllo pastry sheets (approx 14 x 18 inches)
3½ tbsp (50 g) butter, melted

filling:
½ lb (200 g) ground lamb
1 shallot
1 garlic clove
olive oil
1 tsp paprika
½ tsp ground cumin
½ tsp turmeric
4 tbsp chopped parsley
3 tbsp chopped cilantro
½ cup (100 ml) freshly grated parmesan cheese
salt and freshly ground pepper
3 tbsp breadcrumbs
1 small egg yolk

yogurt dip with garlic:
¾ cup (200 ml) yogurt
1–2 garlic cloves, pressed
salt and freshly ground pepper

You almost certainly have come across Asian spring rolls in your life. However, stuffed, delicate rolls are also common in North Africa and in the Middle East. I have chosen ground lamb for my filling, but you can use your imagination and try other things as well. Perhaps a vegetable mix or shellfish. Anything is possible. I usually serve these cigars as a starter, but they're also perfect finger food, as you can eat them while standing.

▨ Follow the instructions on the box to thaw the phyllo sheets. It usually takes about three hours. Be patient, if it doesn't thaw properly, it will crumble into pieces.

▨ Finely chop the shallot and garlic and sauté in olive oil, without browning them. Add the lamb and cook until it's crumbly. Add the dry spices when it's almost done. Remove the pan from the stove and add parsley, cilantro, and cheese. Season to taste with salt and pepper, then, finally, add the breadcrumbs and the egg yolk.

▨ Preheat the oven to 450°F (225°C). Place two phyllo sheets next to each other. Brush the sheets with melted butter, and then place the other two sheets on top. Cut each double sheet in four (making a total of eight rectangles), and brush the edges with some more melted butter.

▨ Spread the filling evenly on the short side of each rectangle. Fold the edges of the long sides toward the middle, and roll it so that it resembles a cigar. Place the rolls on an oven sheet lined with parchment paper, and brush them with melted butter. Bake in the middle of the oven until delicate and golden. This takes about ten minutes.

▨ Serve the cigars fresh from the oven with a dollop of yogurt dip as a starter, on the buffet table, or as finger food with a paper napkin.

BRIK WITH EGG AND TUNA

4 pieces

4 phyllo pastry sheets (approx 14 x 18 inches)
3½ tbsp (50 g) butter, melted, for brushing the pastry

filling:
20 oz (555 g) canned tuna in water
2 shallots
2 tbsp capers, squeezed dry
1 garlic clove, pressed
4 tbsp chopped parsley
1 lemon, zest
approx 1 tsp harissa, store bought or home-made (p. 17)
salt
4 eggs

serve with:
lemon wedges, olives, and a salad

Brik is originally a Tunisian dish, which has become popular all over North Africa. Now it's time for the rest of the world to discover it as well. They are delicate little bundles, like presents, filled with tuna, egg, and capers. I serve them with a salad and some high-quality olives as a starter, for lunch, or as a late-night snack.

▨ Follow the instructions on the packaging to thaw the phyllo sheets. It usually takes about three hours. Be patient, if it doesn't thaw properly, it will fall apart.

▨ Drain the tuna and squeeze out any excess liquid. Chop the shallots and the capers. Mix the tuna, shallots, capers, garlic, parsley, and lemon zest. Season to taste with salt and pepper.

▨ Preheat the oven to 450°F (225°C). Brush two sheets of phyllo with melted butter, and place the other two sheets on top of them. Cut each double sheet in two, and then brush all edges with melted butter.

▨ Place small dollops of filling, slightly off center, on each piece of dough. Make an indent in each dollop of filling and break an egg into each hole. Add a bit of salt and pepper along the eggs. Carefully fold the phyllo over the filling, and seal the edges tightly.

▨ Place the "bundles," with the folded edges facing down, on an oven sheet lined with parchment paper, and brush them with melted butter. Bake in the middle of the oven until the dough has turned golden and crisp. The yolk should still be a little runny. It takes about ten minutes. Serve the briks fresh from the oven.

GREEN SALAD WITH APRICOT AND ORANGE

4 servings

3–5 cups (100–150 g) leafy greens, such as
spinach, chard, beet greens, and dandelion
leaves
6 dried apricots
2 oranges
3 tbsp sunflower seeds
approx ½ cup (100 ml) chopped parsley
approx ¼ cup (50 ml) chopped cilantro
approx ¼ cup (50 ml) chopped mint

dressing:
3 tbsp olive oil
the juice from the 2 oranges
½ tsp ground cumin
½ tsp harissa, store bought or homemade
  (p. 17)
salt

In Morocco, any greens can go in a salad. Piles of leafy greens fill the marketplace. We can learn a lot here; there are so many alternatives to iceberg. Use what you already have. Don't throw away the leaves from your beets, cauliflower, and celery. Fresh herbs are also very good in salads, and swap out the tomato and cucumber for more exciting alternatives. This salad has dried apricots, oranges, and sunflower seeds.

▨ Wash your greens, drain, and pat them completely dry. Inspect the leaves, remove the coarse stems, and tear them using your hands (don't cut them with a knife, as that will create a heavy, compact salad).

▨ Soak the apricots in hot water for about fifteen minutes. Drain and shred.

▨ Peel the oranges with a knife, removing all the white pith. Cut it into membrane-free segments. Save the juices from cutting the oranges for the dressing.

▨ Roast the sunflower seeds in a dry pan.

▨ Mix the ingredients for the dressing.

▨ Mix your greens with the herbs on a large serving plate. Pour most of the dressing over it when it's time to eat (not earlier, as the leaves will collapse), and mix carefully. Spread the oranges and apricots over the salad, drizzle the rest of the dressing over the fruit, and top it off with the sunflower seeds.

TOMATO SALSA

No grilled food in Morocco is ever served without this salsa, be it ground beef, ground lamb, or fish. It is simply irreplaceable. It is slightly different at every restaurant and street food vendor. Some mix it to a smooth tomato sauce, which is good as a dip for bread or as a side to grilled meat. Some chop the tomatoes and onions into large chunks, while others chop them finely. I prefer the latter alternative.

4 servings

2 lbs (1 kg) tomatoes
2 small red onions
2 tbsp freshly squeezed lemon juice
4 tbsp olive oil
4 tbsp chopped cilantro
salt and freshly ground pepper

▨ Cut the tomatoes in half and remove the seeds. Chop the flesh into small cubes. Peel and chop the onion.

▨ Mix all the ingredients together and let the salsa sit for at least an hour before serving. This allows the flavors to blend.

WARM TOMATO SALAD WITH OLIVES

A fresh tomato salad made with flavorful tomatoes tastes wonderful. But during winter, a cold salad isn't always tempting. I make this warm salad with sautéed tomatoes. It goes with pretty much everything. It works as a sauce for burgers at barbecues during the summer, with pasta, in pita bread with grilled vegetables, or simply as a dip for bread. Yum!

4 servings

½ cup (100 ml) high-quality black olives with pits, such as
  kalamata
1–2 anchovy fillets
1 garlic clove, pressed
1 tbsp capers, squeezed dry
½ tsp ground cumin
1½ tbsp olive oil
1 tbsp freshly squeezed lemon juice
approx 10½ oz (300 g) vine tomatoes
olive oil for sautéing
freshly ground pepper
¼ cup (50 ml) chopped parsley

▨ Pit the olives, and mix them with anchovies, garlic, capers, cumin, olive oil, and lemon juice in a food processor. It should make a coarse paste.

▨ Cut the tomatoes into large chunks. Heat some olive oil in a pan and sauté the tomatoes at a low temperature until they start to soften.

▨ Add the olive paste to the pan and let everything simmer for a few minutes. Grind pepper over it. I usually don't add salt because the olives and anchovies are both salty, but that's a matter of preference.

▨ Add the parsley and serve the salad hot or warm.

TOMATO AND PEPPER SALSA

I like condiments that go with everything, and this salsa is just to my taste. It's something in between a salad and a sauce, and can be served hot or cold. Use it as a dip for tasty bread, serve it at a summer barbecue, or pack it in your picnic basket.

4–6 servings

2 onions
3 garlic cloves
3 red bell peppers
1 red chili
1 lb (500 g) tomatoes
olive oil
1 tsp ground cumin
2 tbsp tomato purée
1½ tbsp freshly squeezed lemon juice
1 tsp honey
salt and freshly ground pepper
3 tbsp chopped cilantro

garnish:
black olives

▨ Chop garlic and onions. Dice the peppers. Cut the chili lengthwise, remove the seeds and white ribs, and chop the chili. Chop the tomatoes.

▨ Sauté the onions, garlic, and peppers in olive oil until soft, without browning them. It should take about ten minutes. Add cumin when it's almost done. Add the tomatoes and tomato purée and let simmer until reduced.

▨ Season to taste with lemon juice, honey, salt and pepper, and add the cilantro. Serve the salsa in a bowl topped with olives.

OKRA IN TOMATO SAUCE

Okra can be difficult to get a hold of in some places, especially during winter. If you can't find it fresh or frozen, you can use diced zucchini instead. This vegetable sauce is delicious with anything from burgers to fried fish. Serve it warm or cold; it's your choice. It keeps for a few days in the fridge, and just like most other sauces and stews, the flavor only gets better as the days pass. Read more about okra on p. 19.

4 servings

½ lb (250 g) okra
2 shallots
2 garlic cloves
olive oil
1 tsp ground cumin
14 oz (400 g) canned whole tomatoes
½ cup (100 ml) water
1 vegetable bouillon cube
1 tbsp tomato purée
a dash of cayenne pepper

▨ Chop the shallots and garlic, and sauté in olive oil, without browning them. Add cumin when it's almost done.

▨ Add the tomatoes, and use a pair of scissors to cut the tomatoes into smaller pieces. Add water, the bouillon cube, tomato purée, and cayenne pepper. Cover with a lid and let the sauce simmer for about twenty minutes.

▨ Wash the okra, trim the ends of the stem, and then cut it into inch-long pieces.

▨ Add the okra to the tomato sauce and let it simmer until the okra is soft. It takes about ten minutes. Season to taste. The saltiness from the bouillon is usually enough for my taste, but you might want to add salt. Let the sauce cool.

A Moroccan kitchen offers a sense of community and joy.

MARINATED CARROTS

4 servings

1 lb (500 g) carrots
4 garlic cloves
1 tsp cumin seeds
3 tbsp chopped cilantro or parsley

dressing:
3 tbsp olive oil
½ tsp ground cumin
a dash of harissa, store bought or homemade
(p. 17)
1 tsp paprika
salt

I have never been a fan of cooked carrots, but this recipe has changed my mind.

☒ Peel the carrots and cut into sticks. Peel and chop the garlic.

☒ Add salt, garlic, and cumin seeds to a pot of water and bring to a boil. Let the carrots simmer with a lid on until they start to soften. They shouldn't be mushy. Drain and transfer the carrots to a serving bowl.

☒ Mix all the ingredients for the dressing and pour over the warm carrots. Leave to marinate for at least an hour. Add chopped cilantro or parsley before serving.

WARM CARROT SALAD WITH MANGO

4 servings

1 lb (500 g) carrots
1 shallot
2 garlic cloves
1 mango
2–3 tbsp pistachios
olive oil
1 tbsp freshly grated ginger
1½ tbsp freshly squeezed lemon juice
2 tbsp chopped cilantro
salt

A salad doesn't have to be cold. Skip the raw greens next time and make a delicious stir-fried carrot salad. Served with pork chops, this will add zest to any everyday dinner.

☒ Peel the carrots and cut them into coins. Peel and chop the shallots and garlic. Peel and dice the mango.

☒ Toast the pistachios in a dry pan, and then chop them coarsely.

☒ Sauté the carrots, shallots, and garlic in a bit of olive oil, until the shallots are translucent and the carrots start to soften. Make sure the carrots are still al dente.

☒ Add ginger, lemon juice, and mango, and let it all warm up. Season to taste with salt, and top off with cilantro and pistachios.

BROAD BEAN SALAD WITH MINT

4 servings

4½ lbs (2 kg) fresh broad beans
2 garlic cloves, chopped
4 tbsp olive oil
½ tsp ground cumin
½ tsp lemon zest
½ tbsp freshly squeezed lemon juice
3 tbsp chopped mint
salt and freshly ground pepper

Broad beans are often associated with Italian cuisine, but they are also common in North Africa. It is easiest to find the fresh broad beans for this salad during the summer. Another simple favorite of mine is to eat them boiled, with some extra virgin olive oil, sea salt, and lemon juice, on top of a slice of quality bread.

⊠ Remove the beans from their pods and boil in salted water for about two minutes. Drain and rinse in cold water to cool. Squeeze the beans to remove the white skins. Use a small knife if it's difficult.

⊠ Sauté the garlic in olive oil on low heat, without browning it. Add cumin when it's almost done.

⊠ Add the beans, lemon zest, and lemon juice, and let it all boil for a minute or so. Remove from the heat, add mint and season to taste with salt and pepper. Serve hot, warm, or even cold.

BEET AND ORANGE SALAD

4–6 servings

1⅓ lbs (600 g) fresh beets
2 shallots
1 orange
3 tbsp chopped parsley

dressing:
3 tbsp olive oil
2 tbsp freshly squeezed lemon juice
½ tsp ground cumin
salt and freshly ground pepper

Beets have a natural sweetness, which, together with the orange, gives this salad a wonderful freshness. Another great meeting of flavors is the sweetness of beets with something salty. Try making a Greek version of this salad by adding salty feta cheese.

⊠ Boil the beets in salted water until soft. The amount of time it takes depends on the size of the beets—anywhere from fifteen minutes to an hour. Leave some of the roots and stems on the beets when boiling, to help preserve their flavor and color. Rinse the beets in cold water. While the beets are still warm, gently apply pressure to them until the skin slides off. Let them cool a little and cut them into smaller pieces.

⊠ Peel and chop the shallots. Peel the oranges with a knife, removing all the white pith. Remove the membranes and dice. Mix the beets, shallots, and orange.

⊠ Mix the ingredients for the dressing and pour over the beet salad. Marinate in the fridge for at least an hour. Top with chopped parsley before serving.

ZUCCHINI PICKLE

4–6 servings

2 zucchinis
salt
olive oil for sautéing

marinade:
3 garlic cloves
4 tbsp olive oil
2 tsp freshly grated ginger
1 tsp ground cumin
6 tsp honey
4 tbsp freshly squeezed lemon juice
½ tsp harissa, store bought or homemade
   (p. 17)
salt
3 tbsp chopped parsley
2 tbsp chopped cilantro

"Zucchini in sweet and sour sauce." That's probably the best way to describe this zucchini pickle. The zucchini slices are fried in olive oil, and then soaked in a honey, lemon, and ginger marinade. Make this well in advance, so the flavors have time to develop. When should you serve it? Anytime you would normally serve pickles or chutney. Use it as a condiment for pork chops, put it in lamb burgers, or serve it with chicken. Stuff pita bread with falafel, zucchini pickle, greens, and red onions.

▣ Slice the zucchini. Add a bit of salt and let it sit for about half an hour. Rinse the salt off, pat dry, and fry in olive oil until golden. Let the slices dry on a paper towel.

▣ Chop the garlic and sauté on low heat in olive oil, without browning it. Add ginger, cumin, honey, and lemon juice. Leave to simmer for a few minutes, to create a syrupy marinade. Season to taste with salt and harissa.

▣ Add the zucchini to the marinade and let it simmer for about a minute. Then let it cool before adding the chopped parsley and cilantro. The zucchini should marinate for at least an hour, but the longer the better. It tastes best if you let it marinate for a couple of days in the fridge, but make sure you serve it at room temperature.

VEGETABLE HASH WITH EGGS

4 servings

1 onion
3 garlic cloves
2 red bell peppers
1 zucchini
5 large tomatoes
olive oil
2 tsp paprika
1 vegetable bouillon cube
½ cup chopped parsley
Tabasco
salt
4 eggs

garnish:
paprika
ground cumin
chopped parsley or cilantro

Cooking for one person is always a bit boring. Sometimes it seems like a necessary evil. I'm often in this situation at lunchtime. I'm also a picky eater. I want my food tasty, healthy, and not too heavy (since I have to work in the afternoon as well). In addition, I want my food to be visually appealing, and quick to make. This dish fulfills all my requirements. The vegetables will vary depending on what I have on hand, but the tomatoes are a must, be they fresh or canned.

▣ Chop the onion and the garlic. Dice the peppers and the zucchini. Chop the tomatoes coarsely.

▣ Fry the onion, garlic, peppers, and zucchini in olive oil, in a wide frying pan. Add the paprika toward the end. Add the tomatoes and bouillon and leave to boil until the vegetables are soft, with the lid ajar. It takes about fifteen to twenty minutes. Add parsley and season to taste with Tabasco and salt.

▣ Make four holes in the mixture and crack an egg into each. Put the lid on the pan and let the eggs cook through on low heat, for about five minutes. If you don't put a lid on the pan, the egg yolks will look more appetizing, but they will take longer to cook.

▣ Top with paprika, cumin, and cilantro or parsley.

BROAD BEAN SOUP

4 servings

⅔ lb (300 g) dried broad beans
4 garlic cloves
1 dried chili, crushed
2 tsp ground cumin
1 tsp paprika
2 vegetable bouillon cubes
8½ cups (1½ liters) water
2 tsp freshly squeezed lemon juice
salt

serve with:
yogurt
chopped cilantro

This soup is common street food in Morocco, and is often enjoyed as a heavy breakfast. I personally prefer a different type of breakfast, but I like this broad bean soup a lot for lunch or dinner, with a dollop of yogurt and a slice of tasty bread. Read more about broad beans on p. 19.

▨ Soak the broad beans in cold water overnight, or for at least eight hours. Drain. Transfer the beans to a large pot together with finely chopped garlic, spices, bouillon, and water.

▨ Boil on low heat with a lid on, until the beans are soft and slightly mushy. It takes about an hour.

▨ Use a potato masher to squash the beans. If the soup is too thick, add some more vegetable bouillon or water. Season to taste with salt and lemon juice.

▨ Serve the soup with a dollop of yogurt and some chopped cilantro.

POTATO DUMPLINGS

20 dumplings

2 lbs (800 g) high-starch potatoes
4 garlic cloves
½ cup (100 ml) chopped parsley
3 tbsp chopped cilantro
1½ tsp ground cumin
1½ tsp paprika
1 lemon, zest
salt and freshly ground pepper
2 small eggs
1 tbsp potato flour
sesame seeds and olive oil for frying

serve with:
tomato salsa (p. 36)
high-quality olives
feta cheese

When I was growing up in Sweden, our potato dumplings were always served with a side of bacon and lingonberry jam. Now I've learned to flavor them differently, with different spices, and other condiments. Tomato salsa, feta cheese, and olives are great with these dumplings. They are just as good served room temperature or cold as they are served warm, and because they are also easy to pack up using wax paper, they are a regular part of my picnic basket. What else should you put in the basket? These go great with a Greek salad, grilled chicken, tzatziki, and some quality bread. And there's always room for a bottle of wine and some pie for dessert.

▨ Peel the potatoes and cut into smaller pieces. Put the potatoes and unpeeled garlic cloves into boiling, salted water. Cook for about fifteen minutes, until the potatoes are soft. Drain, and peel the garlic.

▨ Press the potatoes and garlic through a potato ricer into a bowl. Add the rest of the ingredients and mix well.

▨ Leave it in the fridge for a while, to let the flavors develop.

▨ Shape the batter into patties and coat them with sesame seeds. Fry the dumplings in olive oil on both sides, until golden.

BEAN AND SAFFRON STEW

4 servings

2 cups (500 ml) giant white beans
2 cloves
2½ onions
1 packet (½ g) saffron threads
1 tsp turmeric
3 tbsp olive oil
2 cups (500 ml) vegetable broth
½ cup chopped parsley
salt and freshly ground pepper

This is one of the most common dishes served by Moroccan street vendors. I suspect that the saffron is often switched out for turmeric, but I absolutely recommend spending a little more to get the saffron. It adds an amazing flavor to this stew, and it is just as good at the vendor's as it is at home on a cold winter night. It works well on its own as a vegetarian dish, or as a side to salmon or chicken.

⊠ Soak the beans in cold water overnight. Drain. Stick the cloves in the halved onion. Boil the beans on low heat, in salted water together with the halved onion, until they start to soften. It takes about forty minutes. You can choose to use smaller white beans, to shorten the cooking time. Drain the beans.

⊠ Peel the onions and cut into thin wedges. Put beans, onions, saffron, turmeric, olive oil, and broth into a stew pot. Cook on low heat, uncovered, for about half an hour, or until the beans are soft and slightly mushy.

⊠ Add the parsley and flavor to taste with salt and freshly ground pepper.

LENTIL STEW WITH SPINACH AND RAISINS

4 servings

1¼ cups (300 ml) green lentils, such as puy lentils
1 onion
3½ cups (800 ml) water
2 vegetable bouillon cubes
10½ oz (300 g) fresh spinach, preferably baby spinach
⅓ cup (75 ml) sultana raisins
3 tbsp olive oil
½ tsp ground cumin
1 tsp paprika
2 tbsp freshly squeezed lemon juice
approx 2 bunches of cilantro
salt and freshly ground pepper

I like to serve this vegetarian stew with some grilled halloumi. The saltiness of the Cypriot sheep's cheese goes perfectly with the raisins, spinach, and spices in this stew. A tomato salad is also good on the side, not just for the flavor but as a splash of color on the plate. Extra virgin olive oil, red onions, and olives are the tomato salad's best friends.

⊠ Rinse the lentils and drain. Peel and slice the onion thinly. Add lentils, onion, water, and bouillon to a stew pot, add a lid, and cook for about fifteen minutes.

⊠ If you are using regular spinach, be sure to wash it well. Break the leaves into smaller pieces, and remove the thick stems. If you find baby spinach, you can use it as is.

⊠ Add raisins, olive oil, cumin, and paprika to the stew. Fold in the spinach, a little at a time. It will wilt and make room for more. Continue to boil on low heat for about fifteen minutes, until the lentils are soft and the sauce has thickened. Stir occasionally to make sure the spinach mixes with the lentils.

⊠ Add lemon juice and chopped cilantro. Season to taste with salt and pepper.

SWEET POTATO STEW WITH RAISINS AND SAFFRON

4 servings

1 onion
olive oil
1 tsp ground cumin
1 tsp ground ginger
1 tsp paprika
approx 1 packet (½ g) saffron threads
1⅔ cups (400 ml) water
1 vegetable bouillon cube
2 lbs sweet potatoes
⅓ cup (75 ml) raisins
½ cup black olives
14 oz (400 g) canned chickpeas
1 lemon, zest
salt and freshly ground pepper
½ cup (100 ml) chopped cilantro or parsley

serve with:
couscous (p. 59)

This golden yellow stew is just beautiful to look at. What's more important though, is the flavor. It goes with so many things. I like to eat it as a vegetarian dish together with couscous and some crumbled feta cheese, but it is also great with grilled chicken, pork, or salmon. If you want you can use regular potatoes instead of sweet potatoes.

▧ Chop the onion and sauté in some olive oil, without browning it. Add the spices toward the end. Add water and bouillon and bring to a boil.

▧ Peel and dice the potatoes. You want the pieces to be quite large. Add potatoes, raisins, and olives to your stew, and cook until the potatoes are soft. It takes about ten minutes.

▧ Rinse the chickpeas in cold water and drain.

▧ Add the chickpeas and lemon zest to the stew when it's almost ready. Flavor to taste with salt and pepper, and add chopped cilantro or parsley.

EGGPLANT AND DATE STEW

4 servings

1 onion
3 garlic cloves
1 green bell pepper
1 red bell pepper
2 eggplants
1 zucchini
1 lb (500 g) tomatoes
olive oil
1 tbsp paprika
½ cup water
1 vegetable bouillon cube
⅔ cups (150 ml) grated dates, preferably
  fresh
approx 1½ tsp harissa, store bought or
  homemade (p. 17)
salt
½ cup (100 ml) blanched almonds

Dried fruit is the thread that ties Moroccan cuisine together. Try it, enjoy it, be open to learning from other cultures! This is a nice vegetarian stew that I like to serve with couscous or pasta. I eat it with some feta cheese or halloumi, if I happen to have some at home. You can also serve it as a side to chicken, lamb, or pork.

▧ Chop onion and garlic. Cut peppers, eggplant, zucchini, and tomatoes into smaller pieces.

▧ Sauté the onion, garlic, and peppers, without browning them. Add eggplant, zucchini, and paprika, and let it sit for a few minutes. Finally, add the tomatoes.

▧ Add water and bouillon. Leave to simmer with a lid ajar for about twenty minutes, until the vegetables are soft. Add the dates toward the end, about five minutes before the vegetables are done. Season to taste with salt and harissa.

▧ Roast the almonds in a dry pan and sprinkle them over the stew.

COUSCOUS WITH ROASTED VEGETABLES

4 servings

roasted vegetables:
½ cup (50 g) slivered almonds
1 fennel bulb
1 sweet potato
2 red bell peppers
1 red onion
1 zucchini
½ tsp cinnamon
2 tsp dried mint
2 tbsp olive oil
1½ tbsp freshly squeezed lemon juice
salt and freshly ground pepper

couscous:
2 cups (500 ml) couscous
½ cup (100 ml) raisins
2½ cups (600 ml) water
1 vegetable bouillon cube
1 tbsp olive oil
1 lemon, zest

yogurt dip with mint:
¾ cup (200 ml) plain yogurt
2 tbsp chopped mint
1 garlic clove, pressed
salt and freshly ground pepper

Oven roasted veggies. So simple and so tasty. Choose the vegetables you like or whatever is in season, for better taste and better prices. The lemon, cinnamon, and mint give the vegetables a taste of Morocco. Couscous with raisins and a fresh yogurt dip are the perfect companions for this dish.

The vegetables:
▣ Preheat the oven to 450°F (225°C). Roast the almonds in a hot and dry pan.

▣ Inspect your vegetables and chop them into smaller pieces. Spread the vegetables on an oven sheet lined with parchment paper, add cinnamon, mint, and olive oil and mix well. Bake in the middle of the oven until the vegetables are soft. It takes about twenty minutes. Squeeze the lemon juice over them, season to taste with salt and pepper, and top with the toasted almonds.

The couscous:
▣ Put your dry couscous and raisins in a pot with a lid. Bring the bouillon to a boil and pour it over the couscous. Remove from the stove and leave to swell for about five minutes.

▣ Add olive oil and lemon zest and stir the couscous to make it fluffy.

The yogurt dip:
▣ Mix all ingredients and season to taste with salt and pepper.

COUSCOUS WITH DRIED FRUITS

4 servings

approx ¾ cup (200 ml) dried fruit, such as
*   apricots, figs, dates, raisins, and prunes*
2 cups (500 ml) water
1 vegetable bouillon cube
approx ½ packet (¼ g) of saffron threads
1 garlic clove, pressed
1 tsp harissa, store bought or homemade
*   (p. 17)*
1 tsp crushed cardamom seeds
1 lemon, zest
1⅔ cups (300 g) couscous
1½ tbsp olive oil
14 oz (400 g) canned chickpeas
approx ¼ cup (50 ml) chopped pistachios
4 tbsp chopped mint
salt

I know many people think couscous is pretty bland and boring. As always though, you have to know how to use your ingredients. This couscous salad is a favorite of mine with lots of dried fruit, nuts, saffron, mint, and lemon. It's good as a vegetarian dish, which can be served with a dip made from cottage cheese or goat cheese. You can also serve it with chicken or pork. If you're brave enough, serve it as a fresh new dish on the holiday table.

⊠ Soak the dried fruit in hot water for about fifteen minutes. Drain, and cut into smaller pieces.

⊠ Bring water, bouillon, and saffron to a boil. Add garlic, harissa, cardamom, lemon zest, couscous, and dried fruit.

⊠ Remove the pot from the stove and let the couscous swell for about five minutes. Add olive oil and use a fork to stir the couscous fluffy. Let it cool.

⊠ Rinse the chickpeas in cold water and drain. Add chickpeas, nuts, and mint to the couscous, and season to taste with salt.

ROOT VEGETABLE AND PRUNE STEW

4–6 servings

3 red onions
5 garlic cloves
2 large carrots
10 oz (300 g) turnip
10 oz (300 g) celeriac
1 lb (400 g) cabbage
4 tomatoes
olive oil
1 packet (½ g) saffron threads
1 tsp ground ginger
1 tsp paprika
1½ tsp cumin
1 cinnamon stick
3 cups (700 ml) water
3 vegetable bouillon cubes
5 oz (150 g) prunes
½–⅔ cup (100–150 ml) blanched almonds
approx 1 tsp harissa, store bought or home-
     made (p. 17)
salt
¾ cup (200 ml) chopped parsley

serve with:
couscous
harissa, mixed with some bouillon

Root vegetables are great for Moroccan cooking. They go really well with this particular combination of spices: saffron, paprika, ginger, and cumin. Prunes and almonds bring this stew to perfection. Serve it with a light couscous, which will soak up all the bouillon.

※ Peel and cut the onions into wedges. Chop the garlic. Inspect and peel your root vegetables and cabbage, and cut into smaller pieces. Chop your tomatoes into large chunks.

※ Sauté the onion with olive oil in a large pan, without browning it. Add garlic, root vegetables, and cabbage. Add a lid and fry, stirring now and then, until the cabbage has wilted. Add the spices toward the end.

※ Add tomatoes, water, and bouillon, and bring to a boil. Cook on low heat for about thirty-five minutes, or until the vegetables are soft. Add more water if necessary. This stew should have a lot of bouillon when it's finished, almost like a soup.

※ Add the prunes to the stew when the vegetables have about fifteen minutes of cooking time left.

※ Roast the almonds in a dry pan.

※ Season to taste with harissa and salt. Add parsley and top with the almonds.

HOW TO PREPARE COUSCOUS

※ In Morocco, preparing good couscous is a form of craftsmanship. We usually simplify the process by using precooked grains that are ready within minutes. If you want to make a more interesting couscous, there is a recipe for couscous with nuts on p. 56, and another one with raisins and lemon on p. 55. You can read more about couscous on p. 19.

4 servings
※ Pour 2 cups (500 ml) of couscous grains into a bowl. Bring 2 cups (500 ml) of water to a boil together with a vegetable bouillon cube. If you like, also add one tablespoon of olive oil. Pour the bouillon over the couscous and stir. Cover the bowl with a lid and let the grains swell for about five minutes.

※ Stir the couscous with a fork to make it fluffy, and mix in a couple of tablespoons of melted butter. I also like to add a pinch of paprika.

SEVEN VEGETABLE TAJINE

This is one of the more famous tajine dishes. It contains exactly seven types of vegetables, which is supposed to bring you luck. Whether you believe in that kind of thing or not, I feel pretty fortunate when I get to eat vegetarian food that tastes this good.

4–6 servings

2 onions
1 green bell pepper
10 oz (300 g) cabbage
3 firm potatoes
4 carrots
1 zucchini
1 eggplant
3 tomatoes
4 garlic cloves
olive oil
1 tsp crushed coriander seeds
1 tsp ground cumin
1 packet (½ g) saffron threads
3 cups (700 ml) water
3 vegetable bouillon cubes
14 oz (400 g) canned chickpeas
2 tbsp chopped preserved lemon, store
    bought or homemade (p. 68)
1 tbsp freshly squeezed lemon juice
approx 1 tsp harissa, store bought or home-
    made (p. 17)
salt
½ cup (100 ml) chopped cilantro

serve with:
couscous (p. 59)
harissa, mixed with some bouillon

▨ Inspect and peel your vegetables. Cut onions, pepper, cabbage, and potatoes into wedges. Chop the carrots, zucchini, eggplant, and tomatoes into smaller pieces. Chop the garlic.

▨ Sauté onion, garlic, pepper, cabbage, and carrots in a large pan, without browning them. Add the dry spices toward the end.

▨ Add tomatoes and bouillon and bring to a boil. Cook on low heat for about thirty-five minutes, or until the vegetables are soft. Add more water if needed; you want a lot of bouillon when it's done.

▨ When there is about twenty minutes left of the cooking time, add your potatoes, zucchini, and eggplant.

▨ Rinse the chickpeas in cold water and drain. Add the chickpeas and lemon preserves when ten minutes of cooking time remains.

▨ Season to taste with lemon juice, harissa, and salt. Finally, add the cilantro and stir.

BAKED PUMPKIN WITH CARAMELIZED ONION

4–6 servings

3⅓ lbs (1½ kg) pumpkin
salt
2 tbsp water

caramelized onion:
½ cup (100 ml) raisins
approx 16 small shallots
10–12 garlic cloves
2 tbsp butter
2 tbsp canola oil
½ cup (100 ml) blanched almonds
1½ tbsp honey
1½ tbsp freshly squeezed lemon juice
2 tbsp water
¼ tsp cinnamon
1 tsp ground ginger
salt and freshly ground pepper

A dish that is perfect for the fall. The pumpkin wedges are baked in the oven and then glazed with caramelized onion. I sometimes serve this as a main dish with some lemon wedges and couscous, but it's also really good with chicken or pork. Pumpkin is a type of winter squash, which is easiest to find in the fall. Thanks to Halloween, the pumpkin has become popular all over the world.

▩ Preheat the oven to 400°F (200°C). Cut your pumpkin into wedges and remove the skin. You should get about 1¾ lbs (800 g) of pumpkin flesh. Place the wedges in an oven dish, and add salt and water. Cover with aluminum foil and bake in the oven until the pumpkin starts to soften. It takes about half an hour. Drain, and place the pumpkin back in the oven dish.

▩ Soak the raisins in hot water for about fifteen minutes. Drain. Peel the shallots and garlic cloves.

▩ Melt butter with oil in a large pan. Brown the shallots on low heat, then add garlic and almonds. Everything should be browned, but be careful not to burn anything. Add the raisins.

▩ Add honey, lemon, water, cinnamon, and ginger. Bring to a boil. Season to taste with salt and pepper, and remove from the heat.

▩ Pour the onion sauce over the pumpkin wedges and cover with foil. Place the dish back in the oven and bake for fifteen to twenty minutes; until the pumpkin is completely soft.

MEZZE

Socializing around a table filled with various appetizers, or mezze, is something I love. Marinated vegetables, sauces, dips, olives, and whatever else it may be. I like to serve mezze and quality bread at the beginning of a meal, and as an extra course between hors d'oeuvres and the starter. In the summer, I do this at barbecues. Everyone gets a bite of all these different dishes, and then fills up on steak, fish, burgers, and veggies from the grill. You'll find more mezze with tomato on pp. 36–37.

Vegetarian dishes & side dishes   65

TOMATO CONFIT WITH SAFFRON

The Moroccans serve this confit as a mezze at the beginning of a meal. I would describe this as sort of a spicy marmalade or chutney, and recommend you serve it as a condiment with chicken or pork. Sometimes I even serve it with an Italian touch: adding a dollop of it to a crostini, topped with a piece of brie, taleggio, or other aged cheese.

approx 1⅔ cups (400 ml)

2 lbs (800 g) tomatoes
2 shallots
2 tbsp canola oil
1 packet (½ g) saffron threads
1 cinnamon stick
3 tbsp honey
salt and freshly ground pepper

serve with:
crostini
brie or taleggio
toasted sesame seeds

⊠ Cut a cross in the tomatoes, dip them in boiling water, and peel the skins off. Chop into smaller pieces.

⊠ Finely chop the shallots and sauté for a few minutes in olive oil, without browning them. Add tomatoes, saffron, and the cinnamon stick, and leave to simmer for about twenty minutes, without a lid. Stir once in a while.

⊠ Add honey and leave to simmer for another few minutes. Season to taste with salt and pepper. Remove the cinnamon stick and let the marmalade cool. Let it sit in the fridge for at least a day, so that the flavors have time to blend. Serve at room temperature.

SPICY OLIVE DIP

If you like the French tapenade, you should definitely try this. The Moroccan version has different spices and a more oriental flavor.

approx 2¼ cups (300 ml)

2¼ cups (300 ml) pitted olives, such as kalamata
4 garlic cloves, chopped
½ tsp cumin seeds
½ tsp coriander seeds
2 tbsp chopped parsley
2 tbsp chopped cilantro
½ lemon, juice
a dash of chili
¼ cup (100 ml) olive oil

⊠ Mix all the ingredients except for the oil, to make a rough paste. Add the oil and stir.

⊠ Let it sit in the fridge for an hour, so the flavors can blend.

MARINATED OLIVES

There have been olive trees in the area around the Mediterranean since prehistoric times, and they have often been called nature's medicine. I like to snack on these marinated olives with a drink as a different kind of "health food." In moderation, that is.

2¼ cups (300 ml) high quality olives, preferably both black and green
1 red chili, seeded and chopped
2 garlic cloves, thinly sliced
1 tbsp coriander seeds
2 tbsp freshly squeezed lemon juice

⊠ Drain the olives and place them in a bowl. Add the rest of the ingredients and mix well.

⊠ Let the flavors blend for at least two hours, preferably more, before serving.

MINZA—MOROCCAN SALT

⊠ Mix equal parts sea salt with roasted, crushed cumin seeds.

⊠ Try roasting sunflower seeds in a dry pan and mix with some of the salt mix. Good in a salad, or to nibble on with a drink.

EGGPLANT DIP

Eggplant dips, with all sorts of variations, are found in all the Mediterranean countries. You'll get the most flavor out of the eggplant by roasting it first.

approx 2 cups (250 ml)

1½ lbs (700 g) eggplant
2 garlic cloves, chopped
½ tsp ground cumin
1 tsp paprika
3½ tbsp (50 ml) olive oil
1½ tsp freshly squeezed lemon juice
salt and freshly ground pepper

⊠ Preheat the oven to 450°F (225°C). Roast the eggplant in the middle of the oven for half an hour to forty minutes, until it is soft and wrinkly. Turn it a couple of times. Let the eggplant cool, split it and scoop out the flesh.

⊠ Mix all ingredients and season to taste with salt and pepper. Let the flavors develop for at least an hour before serving.

BESSARA

"Bessara" is the name of this broad bean dip, which can be thought of as the hummus of North Africa. This recipe is a bit different from a traditional bessara, as I like to add some fresh herbs. The taste is similar to hummus, and it is served in the same way—with warm bread for dipping.

approx 2 cups (500 ml)

1 cup (250 ml) dried broad beans
2 cloves
½ onion
2 garlic cloves, chopped
¾ tsp ground cumin
3 tbsp chopped cilantro
2 tbsp chopped mint
½ cup (100 ml) olive oil
salt and freshly ground pepper

serve with:
olive oil
roasted sesame seeds

▨ Soak the beans in cold water for at least eight hours. Drain. Stick the cloves in the onion and boil together with the beans, in salted water, on low heat, for about fifty minutes. Drain, but save some of the water for later.

▨ Mix all the ingredients in a food processor and season to taste with salt and pepper. If you find it too thick, add a little bit of the boiling water from the beans.

▨ Let the flavors develop for at least an hour. Drizzle some olive oil over the dip, and top with toasted sesame seeds.

NORTH AFRICAN PESTO

Alright, I know. Calling something pesto in a Moroccan cookbook seems wrong. But I think you'll understand the title. Just like regular pesto, this dip is great on crostini, or to gratinate salmon or chicken fillets.

approx ¾ cup (200 ml)

6–7 cups (200 g) leafy greens, such as spinach, beet leaves, chards, parsley
4 garlic cloves
½ tsp harissa, store bought or homemade (p. 17)
½ tsp ground cumin
1 tbsp chopped cilantro
½ cup (100 ml) olive oil
1 tbsp freshly squeezed lemon juice
salt

▨ Rinse and inspect the greens. Remove all thick stems. Peel and halve the garlic cloves.

▨ Cover the bottom of a pot with salted water and add the greens and the garlic. Cover with a lid and simmer until the greens are wilted and the garlic is soft. Drain and squeeze out all the water, but save some for later.

▨ Mix all ingredients and season with salt. If the pesto is too thick, add a little bit of water from boiling the greens. Let the flavors develop for at least an hour before serving.

EGGPLANT DIP WITH TOMATO

This type of vegetable dish is called a salad in Morocco, but it is really more of a purée. It's great for dipping bread, or together with burgers or falafel.

approx 2 cups (500 ml)

approx 1 lb (500 g) eggplant
salt
olive oil for frying
2 tomatoes
1 large garlic clove, pressed
½ tsp ground cumin
¾ tsp paprika
2 tbsp chopped cilantro
2 tbsp chopped parsley
1½ tsp freshly squeezed lemon juice
freshly ground pepper

▨ Slice the eggplant lengthwise in half-inch thick slices. Add salt and let the eggplant sit for about an hour. Rinse the slices in cold water, pat them dry, and split them in half.

▨ Fry the eggplant in olive oil, until golden on both sides. Put them on some paper towels to dry.

▨ Cut a cross in the tomatoes, dip them in boiling water, and peel the skins off. Split the tomatoes to remove the seeds, and then chop them into smaller pieces.

▨ Mix all the ingredients and season to taste with salt and pepper. Let the flavors develop for at least an hour before serving.

6 small organic lemons
2 + 1 tbsp sea salt
2 cinnamon sticks
3 bay leaves
boiling water
olive oil

PRESERVED LEMONS

These lemons are unique to Moroccan cuisine. Cut thin slices of preserved lemon peel and use it as interesting flavoring in stews, couscous, and salads. It's important that the lemons be small, and also that they are organic, as you are going to be eating the peel. Read more about preserved lemons on p. 21.

▦ Clean a canning jar well, and rinse it with boiling water. Brush the lemons carefully with hot water. Cut every lemon into four wedges, but don't cut them all the way through; they should be attached at one end.

▦ Rub the lemons well with two tablespoons of sea salt, inside and out. Place them in the jar with cinnamon and bay leaves. Add one more tablespoon of salt to the jar, and pour boiling water over them. The lemons should be completely covered in water. If the lemons are not covered, you need to put something on top of them to weigh them down. Pour some olive oil on top as a "seal." Cover with a lid and let the lemons marinate for at least four weeks, preferably longer, at room temperature.

MINT TEA

4 cups (1 liter)

4 cups (1 liter) water
1½ tbsp green tea leaves
a bunch of mint

serve with:
fresh mint
honey or sugar

The national drink of Morocco. According to Moroccan tradition, hosts show hospitality by offering their guests sweet, hot mint tea. The tea is served in silver teapots on silver trays, and is poured into beautiful small glasses.

▦ Pour boiling water over the tea leaves and mint, and leave it for a few minutes.

▦ Pour the tea through a strainer into beautiful glasses designed to withstand heat and add a sprig of mint. Let everyone add honey or sugar to their own taste. North African tea is often sweet.

SAFFRON TEA

4 cups (1 liter)

4 cups (1 liter) water
1½ tbsp green tea leaves
1 packet (½ g) saffron threads

serve with:
lemon slices
fresh mint
honey or sugar

This is another kind of tea, but it is not nearly as common as mint tea. I like to serve this around Christmas, both because it keeps you warm and because I think of saffron as a flavor connected to the holiday season. A small glass of sweet saffron tea is fresh and exciting to serve at the end of a dinner party, perhaps with date cookies (p. 146).

▦ Pour boiling water over the tea leaves and saffron, and leave it for a few minutes.

▦ Pour the tea through a strainer into beautiful glasses designed to withstand heat. Add a slice of lemon and sprig of mint. Let everyone add honey or sugar to their own taste. North African tea is often sweet.

MEAT & POULTRY

CHICKEN STEW WITH FRUITS AND ALMONDS

4 servings

approx 3½ lbs (1½ kg) chicken
1 lemon, juice
salt and freshly ground pepper
2 tsp ground cumin
½ tsp cinnamon
1 packet (½ g) saffron threads
10 prunes, pitted
6 dried apricots
2 onions
⅓ cup (75 ml) sultana raisins
¾ cup (200 ml) water
3 tbsp melted butter
⅔ cup (150 ml) blanched almonds

serve with:
couscous (p. 59) or rice

The Persians contributed a lot to Moroccan cuisine. They used dried fruit in dishes with poultry and meat because they wanted to achieve a contrast between sweet and sour. It symbolized the fight between good and evil. Dried fruit is actually quite delicious in savory food, and not at all strange once you try it.

▨ Preheat the oven to 400°F (200°C). Place the chicken pieces in an ovenproof dish. Sprinkle with lemon juice, and add salt and pepper.

▨ Add cumin and cinnamon to the chicken. Mix the saffron with a little bit of hot water and drizzle it over the chicken.

▨ Soak the prunes and apricots in hot water for about ten minutes. Drain and split in half. Peel the onions and cut them into wedges. Put your dried fruit, onions, and raisins in the dish with the chicken.

▨ Pour the water into the dish and then drizzle the melted butter over the chicken, fruits, and onions.

▨ Cover the dish with aluminum foil. Cook for about thirty-five minutes. Ladle the broth over the chicken a few times while it's baking.

▨ Raise the oven temperature to 450°F (250°C). Remove the foil from the oven dish and bake for another ten minutes, or until the chicken is golden and cooked thoroughly. The chicken is done when the juices are clear.

▨ Roast the almonds in a dry pan, and sprinkle them over the chicken.

meatballs:
1 lb (500 g) ground lamb
2 shallots
2 garlic cloves
½ cup (100 ml) breadcrumbs
1 egg
3 tsp ground cumin
1 tsp salt
½ tsp pepper
4–5 hardboiled eggs
olive oil for frying

tomato sauce:
2 onions
2 garlic cloves
olive oil
28 oz (800 g) canned diced tomatoes
1¼ cups (300 ml) water
2 chicken bouillon cubes
½ cup (100 ml) raisins
1 cinnamon stick
1 tsp honey
salt and freshly ground pepper

serve with:
rice
blanched almonds

LAMB MEATBALLS WITH EGG STUFFING

This is a very different alternative to our classic meatballs. The meat is shaped around a wedge of hard-boiled egg, and then cooked in a full bodied tomato sauce with raisins and cinnamon. It is so exciting to get a taste of other cultures in this manner, and this dish is really delicious.

The meatballs:
▨ Chop onions and garlic finely.

▨ Mix all the ingredients for the meatballs except for the hard-boiled eggs. Let the flavors settle for a while in the fridge.

▨ Peel the eggs and cut them into wedges. Shape the meat into 16 relatively large meatballs, and then press down to flatten them. Put a piece of egg on each one, fold the meat over it, and shape into a ball again. Try to get an even surface. If there are pieces of egg left over, save them for garnish.

▨ Brown the meatballs in olive oil, then add half of them to the tomato sauce. Stir a couple of times. Cook for ten to fifteen minutes, remove from sauce, and cook the rest.

The tomato sauce:
▨ Chop onions and garlic and sauté in a large pan, without browning them. Add tomatoes, water, bouillon, raisins, cinnamon, and honey.

▨ Cover with a lid and let the sauce cook for fifteen to twenty minutes. Season to taste with salt and pepper.

The rice:
▨ Cook the rice, following the directions on the package.

▨ Roast the blanched almonds in a hot and dry pan.

▨ Top the rice with the almonds.

OKRA AND LAMB STEW

A stew with meat and vegetables sounds pretty common, but okra is quite special. Sometimes, finding it fresh can be hard, but try large supermarkets or Middle Eastern markets. If you can't find it fresh, look for it frozen. Read more about okra on p. 19.

4–6 servings

approx 2 lbs (1 kg) lamb meat, boneless
olive oil
salt and freshly ground pepper
2 onions
3 garlic cloves
1 yellow bell pepper
1 red bell pepper
1 tsp paprika
1 cinnamon stick
1 tbsp freshly grated ginger

2 cups water
3 tbsp veal stock (buy at a specialty food store, or substitute with 2 beef bouillon cubes)
½–⅔ lb (200–300 g) okra
2 tomatoes
½ cup (100 ml) blanched almonds

serve with:
couscous (p. 59) or rice

⊠ Cut the meat into one-inch cubes. Brown it a little at a time in olive oil. Add salt and pepper and set aside.

⊠ Cut the onions into wedges and chop the garlic. Cut the peppers into smaller pieces.

⊠ Fry the onions, garlic, and peppers with olive oil, in a stew pot. Add the spices toward the end. Add the meat to the pot, pour in the water and veal stock, cover with a lid, and cook over low heat for about an hour. Stir every once in a while.

⊠ Rinse the okra and remove the stems. Cut the tomatoes into wedges. Add the okra and tomatoes to the stew. Cook for about fifteen minutes, until the okra is soft and the meat is tender. Season to taste with salt and pepper.

⊠ Meanwhile, toast the almonds, and top the stew with them when it's ready.

MERGUEZ AND LAMB STEW

Is there anything better than stew simmering on the stove? On cold winter nights, the sight and smell alone is enough to keep you warm. This stew is given an extra kick from the spicy lamb sausage, merguez. This can be hard to find. If you don't find any at your local ethnic market, you can use a nice chorizo or another spicy sausage of your choosing.

4–6 servings

approx 2 lbs (1 kg) lamb meat, boneless
olive oil
salt and freshly ground pepper
2 onions
4 garlic cloves
1 large carrot
1 packet (½ g) saffron threads
1 tsp ground cumin or ras el hanout (p. 23)
1 tsp ground ginger
1 tsp paprika
4 cups (1 liter) water

3 tbsp veal stock (buy at a specialty food store, or substitute with 2 beef bouillon cubes)
1 lb (500 g) firm potatoes
14 oz (400 g) canned chickpeas
½ lb (500 g) merguez, or other spicy sausage
½ cup (100 ml) chopped parsley
½ cup (100 ml) chopped cilantro

serve with:
tasty bread

⊠ Cut the meat into one-inch cubes. Brown it, a little at a time, in olive oil. Add salt and pepper and set aside.

⊠ Slice the onions and chop the garlic. Peel and dice the carrot finely.

⊠ Sauté the vegetables with olive oil, in a large stew pot, without browning them. Add the spices when they're almost done. Add the meat to the pot, pour in the water and veal stock, cover with a lid, and cook over low heat for about an hour.

⊠ Peel and chop the potatoes coarsely. Rinse and drain the chickpeas.

⊠ Add potatoes and sausage to the pot and cook for another fifteen minutes. Add the chickpeas when only a few minutes remain.

⊠ Remove the sausage, cut it into smaller pieces, and return them to the stew. Season to taste with salt and pepper, add the herbs, and stir.

CHICKEN WITH SWEET POTATO AND RAISINS

4 servings

1 large chicken, at least 3⅓ lbs (1½ kg).
salt and freshly ground pepper
1 large onion
1 packet (½ g) saffron threads
1 tsp paprika
1 tsp ground ginger
1 cinnamon stick
2 cloves
1 chicken bouillon cube
2–3 tbsp melted butter
2 cups water
1½ lbs (750 g) sweet potatoes
⅔ cup (150 ml) sultana raisins
½ cup (100 ml) parsley

Chicken, potatoes, and sauce. Everything in one pot, taking care of itself in the oven. Does it get any better?

⊠ Preheat the oven to 400°F (200°C). Add salt and pepper to the chicken. Peel and finely slice the onion. Put the onion, spices, and the bouillon cube into an ovenproof pot and mix well. Add the chicken and brush it with melted butter. Add the water.

⊠ Cover with a lid and cook in the oven for about an hour. Ladle the broth over the chicken a few times while it's baking.

⊠ Raise the oven temperature to 450°F (250°C). Remove the lid and continue to cook for another fifteen minutes, or until the chicken is done. It should have a golden coloring and the juices should be clear.

⊠ Remove the chicken from the pot and keep it warm in aluminum foil. Remove the cinnamon stick. Peel and chop the sweet potatoes coarsely. Add potatoes and raisins to the sauce and cook without a lid until the potatoes are soft. It takes about fifteen minutes. Season to taste with salt and pepper, and add the parsley.

⊠ Cut the chicken up into eight pieces and serve together with the potatoes.

LAMB SOUP WITH COUSCOUS AND DRIED FRUIT

6 servings

10–15 oz (300–400 g) lamb meat,
*   boneless*
2 onions
4 garlic cloves
1 red bell pepper
5 tomatoes
1 chili
10 dried apricots
olive oil
2 tsp ground cumin
3 tsp dried mint
8½ cups (2 liters) water
4 beef bouillon cubes
¼ cup (50 ml) raisins
14 oz (400 g) canned chickpeas
¼ cup (50 ml) couscous
approx ½ tsp harissa, store bought or home-
*   made (p. 27)*
1 tbsp freshly squeezed lemon juice
salt
½ cup (100 ml) chopped parsley
3½ tbsp (50 ml) chopped mint

I love soup. When I was little, I did not at all like the meat broth I was usually served, but that was a long time ago! This meat soup, with lovely spices, vegetables, and fruit, is delicious and full of flavor. The ingredients go perfectly together. It's a rich soup that will satisfy your hunger and warm you up.

▦ Trim the meat, removing all the sinew and unwanted fat, and cut it into small pieces.

▦ Cut the onion and the tomatoes into wedges, and chop the garlic. Dice the pepper. Split the chili in half, remove the seeds and white veins, and chop it finely. Shred the apricots.

▦ Sauté the onion, garlic, and pepper in olive oil, in a large pot, without browning them. Add the meat and brown it on all sides. Add cumin and dried mint when it's almost done.

▦ Add water and bouillon, bring to a boil and skim the fat. Cover with a lid and cook for about forty minutes, or until the meat is very tender.

▦ Add tomatoes, chili, raisins, and apricots when half the cooking time has passed.

▦ Rinse and drain the chickpeas. Add to the soup when there is about five minutes left.

▦ Season to taste with harissa, lemon juice, and salt. Add the herbs.

MEATBALLS IN TOMATO SAUCE

In Sweden, where I am from, we like to believe that we invented meatballs. We are very wrong. Meatballs are popular all over the world. I cook these meatballs directly in the tomato sauce. The best part about that? You get a mouthwatering scent in the house instead of that horrible fried meat smell.

4 servings

meatballs:
1 lb (500 g) ground lamb
½ onion
2 garlic cloves, pressed
1 egg
1 tsp salt
½ tsp ground cumin or ras el hanout (p. 23)
1 lemon, zest
3 tbsp chopped cilantro

tomato sauce:
1 onion
2 garlic cloves
olive oil
1 tbsp tomato purée
28 oz (800 g) canned diced tomatoes
½ cup (100 ml) water
2 chicken bouillon cubes
½ tsp ground cumin
1 cinnamon stick
14 oz (400 g) canned chickpeas (optional)
salt and freshly ground pepper
chopped parsley

serve with:
couscous (p. 59), pasta, or rice

The meatballs:

▣ Peel and chop the onion. Mix all the ingredients for the meatballs and let the flavors develop for a while in the fridge. Shape the meat into 12 large balls.

The tomato sauce:

▣ Chop the onion and garlic and sauté in olive oil for a few minutes, without browning them. Add tomato purée, diced tomatoes, water, bouillon, cumin, and cinnamon. Leave to simmer for about twenty minutes.

▣ Place half of the meatballs in the tomato sauce, and cook over low heat for about fifteen minutes. Turn them around a few times. Remove from the sauce and repeat with the rest of the meatballs. When they're ready, place all meatballs back in the sauce.

▣ Rinse and drain the chickpeas, and add them to the sauce. Season to taste with salt and pepper, and top with some chopped parsley.

MY MOROCCAN BOLOGNESE

Dried fruit, almonds, and lamb meat are typical ingredients in Moroccan cuisine. This is my Moroccan version of a Bolognese.

4 servings

approx 1 lb (500 g) ground lamb or pork
1 large onion
3 garlic cloves
1 red chili
olive oil
2 tsp paprika
1 packet (½ g) saffron threads

1 cinnamon stick
1 tbsp freshly grated ginger
1 tsp ground cumin
14 oz (400 g) canned diced tomatoes
3/4 cup (200 ml) water
1 chicken bouillon cube
14 oz (400 g) canned chickpeas (optional)

3½–5 oz (100–150 g) prunes
salt and freshly ground pepper

serve with:
couscous (p. 59), pasta, or rice

▣ Chop onion and garlic. Split the chili in half, remove seeds and white veins, and chop finely.

▣ Sauté the onion and garlic without browning them. Add the minced meat and chili and cook until browned. Add the spices when it's almost done. Add tomatoes, water, and bouillon, and bring to a boil. Cover with a lid and let the sauce simmer for about twenty minutes.

▣ Rinse the chickpeas in cold water, and drain. Split the prunes. Add the chickpeas and prunes to the sauce and cook, without the lid, for another ten minutes. Season to taste with salt and pepper.

CHICKEN STEW WITH POTATOES AND OLIVES

4 servings

approx 3¼ lbs (1½ kg) chicken
butter
salt and freshly ground pepper
1 large onion
3 garlic cloves
4 tomatoes
1 tsp turmeric
1 tsp ground cumin or ras el hanout (p. 23)
½ tsp crushed coriander seeds
2½ cups (600 ml) water
1½ lbs (700 g) firm potatoes
2 tbsp preserved lemon, store bought or
*   homemade (p. 68), chopped*
½ cup (100 ml) large green olives, with pits
3 tbsp chopped parsley
3 tbsp chopped cilantro

serve with:
quality bread

This is one version of classic chicken with preserved lemons. The preserved lemons add an interesting flavor, as they always do, and they are difficult to substitute with something else. The potatoes are cooked in the stew as well, so the only thing needed on the side is a slice of bread. Read more about preserved lemons on pp. 21 and 68.

▦ Add butter to a frying pan and brown the chicken on all sides. Add salt and pepper and set aside.

▦ Slice the onion, and chop the garlic and tomatoes.

▦ Add some butter to a stew pot and sauté the onion and garlic, without browning them. Add the spices toward the end. Add tomatoes and water and let the sauce simmer for a few minutes.

▦ Add the chicken to the pot and cook in the sauce until it's cooked through. It takes about forty-five minutes. You know that the chicken is ready when the juices are clear.

▦ Peel and chop the potatoes coarsely. Add potatoes, preserved lemons, and olives to the stew when there is about fifteen minutes of cooking time remaining. Cook until the potatoes are soft. Season to taste with salt and pepper, and add the fresh herbs.

LAMB STEW WITH APRICOTS AND ALMONDS

4 servings

1½ lbs (700 g) lamb meat, boneless
olive oil
salt and freshly ground pepper
1 onion
3 garlic cloves
2 celery stalks
1½ tsp ground cumin
½ tsp crushed coriander seeds
1 packet (½ g) saffron threads
2 tsp paprika
1 cinnamon stick
1½ tbsp freshly grated ginger
1½ tbsp veal stock (buy at a specialty food store, or substitute with a beef bouillon cube)
2 cups (500 ml) water
5 oz (150 g) dried apricots
½ cup (100 ml) blanched almonds
1 tbsp freshly squeezed lemon juice
approx 1 tsp harissa, store bought or home-made (p. 27)
4 tbsp chopped cilantro

serve with:
couscous (p. 59)

Dried fruit, almonds, and flavorful spices are typical for the Moroccan meat stews. If you can't go to Morocco, at least you can enjoy a deliciously warming lamb stew.

Cut the meat into one-inch cubes. Brown, a little at a time, in a pan with olive oil. Add salt and pepper and set aside.

Chop onion and garlic and slice the celery. Add olive oil to a stew pot and sauté, without browning them. Add the spices towards the end.

Add the meat, veal stock, and water to the pot. Cover with a lid and cook over low heat for about an hour. Stir every once in a while.

Soak the apricots in hot water for ten minutes. Drain. Roast the almonds in a dry pan.

Add the apricots to the stew and continue cooking for about twenty minutes, until the meat is tender and the apricots are soft. Season to taste with lemon juice, harissa, and salt. Add the cilantro and top with almonds.

HARIRA—RAMADAN MEAT SOUP

6 servings

10–14 oz (300–400 g) veal or lamb meat,
   boneless
2 onions
9 oz (250 g) celeriac
1 carrot
3 tomatoes
olive oil
1 tsp paprika
1 tsp ground ginger
1 packet (½ g) saffron threads
8½ cups (2 liters) water
4 tbsp veal stock (buy at a specialty food
   store, or substitute with 2 to 3 beef
   bouillon cubes)
14 oz (400 g) canned chickpeas
¾ cup (200 ml) red lentils
approx 1 tsp harissa, store bought or homemade (p. 27)
salt
½ cup (100 ml) chopped parsley
½ cup (100 ml) chopped cilantro

serve with:
hard-boiled eggs
paprika
shredded dates, preferably fresh

This soup is a Moroccan classic. Every night during Ramadan the fast is broken with a handful of dates, followed by a plate of Harira. It is an appetizing and filling soup Every housewife has her own recipe. Personally, I need no excuse to eat this flavorful, delicious soup any time of the year. An unexpected but great combination is to serve this soup with hard-boiled eggs and shredded dates.

▨ Trim the meat of any sinews, and cut into small pieces.

▨ Peel the onion and cut into thin wedges. Peel and dice the root vegetables finely. Chop the tomatoes.

▨ Sauté the onion and root vegetables in a large stew pot, without browning them. Add the meat and brown on all sides. Add the spices when it's almost done.

▨ Add tomatoes, water, and veal stock. Bring to a boil, and skim the fat. Add a lid and cook for about forty minutes, until the meat is very tender.

▨ Rinse the chickpeas in cold water and drain. Add chickpeas and lentils to the soup and boil until the lentils are soft and start to get mushy. It takes about ten minutes. Season to taste with harissa and salt, and add the herbs.

▨ When time to serve: Split the hard-boiled eggs, one for each person, and season them with paprika. Let your guests garnish their own soup with a piece of egg and shredded dates.

TURKEY AND FIG STEW

4 servings

1½ lbs (700 g) turkey breast fillet
butter
salt and freshly ground pepper
4 dried figs
2 onions
1 cinnamon stick
1½ tsp ground ginger
1½ tsp turmeric
2½ cups (600 ml) water
1 chicken bouillon cube
1 lb (500 g) sweet potatoes or regular
  potatoes
½ cup (100 ml) chopped parsley
½ cup (100 ml) blanched almonds
4 fresh figs

serve with:
couscous (p. 59), or rice

Whole turkey is something so completely associated with Thanksgiving that it can seem weird to buy it at other times of the year. But turkey meat has many possibilities. It is tasty, juicy, and lean. Buying a turkey breast fillet should be just as common as buying chicken. The turkey breast fillet is easy to cook, and is perfect in a stew.

▨ Chop the turkey meat into smaller pieces. Add butter to a frying pan and brown, a little at a time. Add salt and pepper and set aside.

▨ Soak the dried figs in hot water for about ten minutes. Drain, remove the stems, and split in half.

▨ Cut the onion into thin wedges and sauté in butter, in a stew pot, without browning it. Add the spices when it's almost done.

▨ Add the turkey, dried figs, water, and bouillon to the pot, and cook over low heat for about fifteen minutes.

▨ Meanwhile, peel your potatoes and chop them coarsely. Add the potatoes to the stew and cook for another ten to fifteen minutes, until the potatoes are soft. Add parsley, and season to taste with salt and pepper.

▨ Roast the blanched almonds in a dry pan.

▨ Cut each fresh fig into four pieces and add them to the stew. Push them gently into the stew so that they are soaked in the sauce. Cover the pot and let it sit for about two minutes, until the figs are warm. Top with the almonds.

Pastilla

This dish was created in the kitchens of the royal court and is considered the national dish of Morocco. It's a pie with pigeon stuffing and a delicate phyllo crust. The Moroccans love sweet things in their food, so the pastilla is topped with cinnamon and powdered sugar.

I personally don't like powdered sugar on my food, and honestly, I don't like pastilla. That's why you will have to make do with a picture of this dish (p. 98). I might add that Ove, my beloved husband, almost passed out one warm night in a restaurant when he was forced to eat pastilla for dinner.

MOROCCAN CASSOULET

The inspiration for this stew is the French classic from Languedoc. It is a must if you're a fan of lamb and white beans, and it is perfect when you need to serve a lot of guests. You only need this stew and some bread. Oh, and a fine red wine, preferably from the south of France.

6–8 servings

1¼ cups (300 ml) dried
   giant white beans
2¼ lbs (1 kg) lamb or pork
   stew meat
olive oil
salt and freshly ground
   pepper
2 onions
4 garlic cloves
2 cloves
1 cinnamon stick
1 packet (½ g) saffron threads

1 tsp ground cumin
1 tsp paprika
1 tbsp thyme
2 bay leaves
1 tbsp tomato purée
14 oz (400 g) canned
   whole tomatoes
2½ cups (600 ml) water
2 tbsp veal stock (buy at
   a specialty food store, or
   substitute with a beef
   bouillon cube)

1 orange, zest
½ lb (300 g) merguez, or
   other spicy sausage
½–1 tsp harissa, ready or
   homemade (p. 27)

serve with:
good bread

▣ Soak the beans in cold water for about ten hours, or overnight. Drain.

▣ Cut the meat into one-inch cubes. Brown in a frying pan with olive oil, a little at a time. Add salt and pepper, and set aside.

▣ Chop the onions and garlic, and fry with olive oil in a large stew pot. Add the spices when it's almost done. Add tomato purée, tomatoes, water, and veal stock. Peel the washed orange with a potato peeler, and add the peel to the stew.

▣ Add the meat and beans. The water should be just enough to cover it. Cover with a lid and cook until the meat is tender and the beans are soft. It takes about an hour and fifteen minutes.

▣ When there is twenty minutes left, add the sausage. Season to taste with salt and harissa mix. Remove the orange peel. Take the sausage out, cut it into smaller pieces, and return it to the stew.

VEAL SHANK WITH RAISINS

I like to use veal shank for stews, as it makes a really good full-bodied bouillon. One classic is osso buco, the Italian veal stew with tomato sauce. I like to try new things though, and this is my Moroccan version.

approx 3½ lbs (1½ kg)
   veal shank, or lamb
   shank, cutlets
olive oil
salt and freshly ground
   pepper
1 onion
3 garlic cloves
1 carrot
approx 3½ oz (100 g)
   celeriac
2 tsp paprika

½ packet (¼ g) saffron
   threads
1 cinnamon stick
1 tsp chili powder
1 tsp ground ginger
1 tsp ground cumin
14 oz (400 g) canned
   whole tomatoes
1⅓ cups (300 ml) water
2 tbsp veal stock (buy at
   a specialty food store, or
   substitute with a beef

bouillon cube)
1 tbsp tomato purée
½ orange, zest
½ cup (100 ml) sultana
   raisins
½ cup (100 ml) chopped
   parsley

serve with:
a creamy risotto, pasta, or
   couscous (p. 59)

▣ Add olive oil to a frying pan and brown the meat on both sides. Add salt and pepper and set aside.

▣ Chop the onion and garlic. Peel the carrot and celeriac, and dice finely. Sauté the onion, garlic, carrot, and celeriac in a stew pot with olive oil, without browning them. Add the spices toward the end.

▣ Add tomatoes, water, veal stock, and tomato purée, and bring to a boil. Peel the washed orange with a potato peeler, and add the peel to the stew.

▣ Add the meat to the tomato sauce, cover with a lid, and cook over low heat until the meat is tender. It takes about an hour and a half. Ladle the sauce over the meat a few times.

▣ Add the raisins after about half the cooking time has passed. Season to taste with salt and pepper, and top with parsley.

QUAIL WITH APRICOTS

4 servings

4 large or 8 small quail (can be substituted with Cornish hens)
salt and freshly ground pepper
butter
1 onion
1½ tsp ground ginger
½ packet (¼ g) saffron
2 cloves
1 cinnamon stick
2 cups (500 ml) water
1 chicken bouillon cube
8–10 dried apricots
3 tbsp apricot jam

serve with:
mashed potatoes, or oven baked potato wedges

Moroccan cooking is partly influenced by French cuisine because the nation was once a French colony. Quail is common in French cooking, and here I've made it with a Moroccan twist.

▢ Add salt and pepper to the quail, and make sure it's everywhere; inside and out. Brown them on all sides with butter in a frying pan. Set aside.

▢ Peel and slice the onion finely. Melt some butter in a stew pot, large enough for the quail. Add the onions and sauté for a few minutes, without browning them. Add the spices toward the end. Add water and bouillon, and bring to a boil.

▢ Add the quail (or Cornish hens) to the pot, cover with a lid, and cook slowly for about thirty minutes. Ladle bouillon over the birds, and turn them a couple of times.

▢ Soak the apricots in hot water for about fifteen minutes. Drain and split them in half.

▢ Add the apricots and the jam to the stew, and cook for another ten minutes. Season to taste with salt and pepper.

LAMB KEBABS

4 servings

1 lb (500 g) ground lamb or pork
½ small onion, finely chopped
2 garlic cloves, pressed
½ tsp pepper
1 tsp paprika
1 tsp ground cumin
¼ cup (50 ml) chopped parsley
¼ cup (50 ml) chopped cilantro
1 tsp salt
1 egg
8–12 skewers

When the sun sets, Jemaa el Fnaa Square in Marrakech is transformed into a large barbecue party, filled with vendors serving all sorts of food—most of it coming from the grill. The smoke lies heavily over the square. If you are ever in Marrakech, you have to have at least one meal here. The food is extraordinary and cheap. Jesters, snake-charmers, and fortune-tellers . . . all the entertainment you can ask for is right here. It's no coincidence that this square is sometimes called Jester's Square. However, you don't need to go to Morocco to enjoy these tasty lamb kebabs. Have a barbecue and serve these with a selection of salads, mezze, dips, and olives.

Mix the ground meat thoroughly with the rest of the ingredients. Let the flavors mix together for at least an hour in the fridge.

If you are using wooden skewers, soak them in cold water for a while so they won't burn easily. Preheat the oven to 450°F (250°C), using the grill setting, or fire up your barbecue.

Shape the meat into sausage-like rolls, and stick the skewers through them. Place them on an oven sheet greased with oil.

Grill the skewers high in the oven for about five minutes, turn them, and grill for another five minutes. The exact time varies depending on the thickness of the kebabs, and whether you want them pink on the inside, or well-done; pork should not be pink on the inside. You can also cook the skewers on the barbecue grill.

MARINATED LAMB SKEWERS

4 servings

approx 1⅓ lbs (600 g) lamb meat, boneless
salt and freshly ground pepper
8 skewers

marinade:
1 tbsp olive oil
1 tsp turmeric
1 tsp ground cumin
2 garlic cloves, pressed
1 tbsp chopped mint
1 tbsp chopped cilantro
1 tbsp chopped parsley

In Morocco the marinades are dry, without lots of olive oil. I believe we have a lot to learn from this. Too much oil will cause the grill to flare up when the marinade drips onto the grill. Or at least it does when I'm barbecuing. This marinade is great for other meats as well, not just for lamb. You can serve these skewers with the same sides as the lamb kebabs.

Mix the ingredients for the marinade. Cut the meat into slightly smaller than one-inch cubes Pat the meat with the spice mix and marinate for at least two hours.

If you are using wooden skewers, soak them in cold water for a while so they won't burn easily. Preheat the oven to 450°F (250°C), using the grill setting, or fire up your barbecue.

Thread the meat on the skewers and place them on an oven sheet greased with oil.

Grill the skewers high in the oven for about five minutes, turn them, and grill for another five minutes. The exact time depends on whether you want your meat pink on the inside, or well-done. Add salt and pepper to taste. You can also cook the skewers on the barbecue.

CHICKEN WITH PRESERVED LEMON AND OLIVES

4 servings

1 large chicken, at least 3⅓ lbs (600 g)
2 tbsp olive oil
2 garlic cloves, chopped
1 tsp ground ginger
1 tsp ground cumin
1 tsp paprika
1 packet (½ g) saffron threads
1 cinnamon stick
salt and freshly ground pepper
2 onions
1 bunch of mint
1 bunch of cilantro stalks
2 cups (500 ml) water
2 tbsp chopped preserved lemon (p. 68)
1 tbsp freshly squeezed lemon juice
approx ½ cup (100 ml) large green olives
  with pits

serve with:
couscous (p. 59) or rice

This is one of Morocco's most famous dishes, which you will stumble upon everywhere you go: in the street, in private homes, and in restaurants. The preserved lemons and the olives give the sauce a very special taste. It's both fresh and salty. When returning from Morocco, you'll see that this special lemony taste lingers in your mouth for days.

▣ Preheat the oven to 400°F (200°C). Rub the chicken with olive oil. Mix garlic, spices, salt, and pepper in a stew pot. Add the chicken and pat it all over with the spice mix.

▣ Peel and slice the onion finely. Add the onion, and the stalks from the parsley and cilantro. Pour in the water.

▣ Cover the pot with a lid and cook in the oven for about an hour. Ladle the sauce over the chicken a few times.

▣ Increase the oven temperature to 450°F (250°C). Remove the lid from the pot and cook for about fifteen minutes more, until the chicken takes on a golden coloring. You know that the chicken is ready when the juices are clear.

▣ Remove the chicken from the pot and keep it warm in aluminum foil. Remove the herb stalks and the cinnamon stick, and skim any fat off the surface.

▣ Add preserved lemon, lemon juice, and olives, and let the sauce simmer on the stove for about fifteen minutes. Season to taste with salt and pepper.

▣ Cut the chicken into eight pieces, return it to the sauce, and heat it up.

ROASTED LAMB WITH LEMON AND MINT

6 servings

1 leg of lamb, bone-in, approx 4½ lbs
    (2 kg)
4 garlic cloves
salt and freshly ground pepper

marinade:
2 garlic cloves, chopped
1 lemon, zest
3 tbsp freshly squeezed lemon juice
4 tbsp olive oil
4 tbsp chopped mint
2 tsp ground cumin
1 tsp harissa, store bought
    or homemade (p. 27)

Whole spit-roasted lamb is often served on special occasions. I think a leg is more than enough. Serve this with a few different salad options, the dips and salsas on pp. 36–37 and 66–67, or perhaps with a nice au gratin made of potatoes or other vegetables.

▨ Trim the meat. Peel the garlic cloves and split them in half, lengthwise. Using a sharp knife, make little slits all over the lamb and stuff it with garlic.

▨ Mix the ingredients for the marinade. Stir by hand until the mixture is well blended and smooth. Put the lamb with the marinade inside double plastic bags. Marinate for a few hours, or overnight.

▨ Preheat the oven to 350°F (175°C). Add salt and pepper to the meat. Stick a meat thermometer into the thickest part of the meat, but be careful not to hit the bone. Place the leg in a roasting pan (line it with parchment paper if you like).

▨ Cook in the middle of the oven until the thermometer shows 152°F (67°C) degrees for medium, or 161°F (72°C) for well-done.

▨ Remove the lamb from the oven and wrap it in aluminum foil. The temperature will rise a few more degrees. Slice the meat finely before serving.

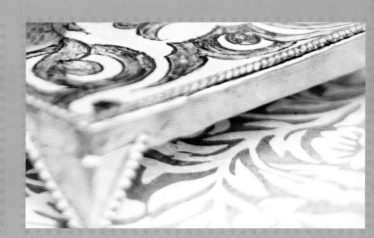

BAKED FISH WITH TOMATOES AND OLIVES

4 servings

2 scaled and gutted fish, such as pike-perch,
  each approx 2 lbs (800 g)
1 big bunch of parsley
2 tomatoes
salt
⅔ cup (150 ml) large olives, with pits

marinade:
1 tsp cumin seeds
1 tsp rough salt
½ tsp paprika
½ tsp chili powder
5 garlic cloves
3 tbsp chopped cilantro
1 tbsp grated onion
6 tbsp olive oil
1 tbsp freshly squeezed lemon juice

What is available at the fish counter can vary a lot depending on where you live. You can choose any type of fish you like for this dish. I chose rose fish, a beautiful pink fish from the North Sea, caught outside the Swedish coast of Bohus.

▣ Start with the marinade. Roast the cumin seeds in a dry pan. Crush the seeds with salt, paprika, chili powder, garlic, and cilantro, using a mortar and pestle. Add grated onion, olive oil, and lemon juice. Mix to make a sauce.

▣ Rinse the fish in cold water and dry them. Pat them well, on the inside as well as the outside, with the marinade. Save about four tablespoons of the marinade for later. Marinate the fish for at least two hours at room temperature, or longer in the fridge.

▣ Preheat the oven to 400°F (200°C). Cover a greased ovenproof dish with parsley, and place the fish on top. Slice the tomatoes and cover the fish with the slices. Drizzle the remaining marinade on top, and put the olives inside and around the fish.

▣ Bake in the middle of the oven for about twenty-five minutes.

SEAFOOD SOUP

4 servings

approx 1 lb (500 g) fillet of white fish, such
* as halibut*
1 lb (500 g) shrimp, in their shells
approx 1 lb (500 g) mussels

the soup:
2 onions
4 garlic cloves
2 celery stalks
1 red chili
4 tomatoes
olive oil
½ tsp ground cumin
2 tsp paprika
1 packet (½ g) saffron threads
6½ cups (1½ liters) water
3 chicken bouillon cubes
2 tbsp freshly squeezed lemon juice
Tabasco
salt
3 firm potatoes
½ cup (100 ml) chopped parsley
4 tbsp chopped cilantro

serve with:
orange aioli with a kick
quality bread

2 garlic cloves
2 egg yolks
⅔ cup (150 ml) canola oil
½ cup (100 ml) olive oil
a pinch of orange zest
a dash of sambal oelek
salt

Fish soup is always delicious. It's great for when you have guests, as you can prepare the soup the day before, and just add the fish and shellfish when it's time to serve. You'll want some high-quality bread to serve on the side. Add a dollop of aioli to create the perfect finishing touch.

⊠ Cut the onion into fine wedges. Chop the garlic and slice the celery. Split the chili in two, remove the seeds and white veins, and slice finely. Cut the tomatoes coarsely.

⊠ Add olive oil to a large stew pot and sauté the onion, garlic, celery, and chili, without browning them. Add the spices toward the end. Add tomatoes, water, and bouillon, and cover with a lid on for about half an hour. Season to taste with lemon juice, Tabasco, and salt. If you aren't serving the soup until the next day, here is a good place to stop and pick up later.

⊠ Peel the potatoes and cut into smaller pieces. Add them to the soup and cook for about ten minutes.

⊠ Dice the fish and scale the shrimp. Brush the mussels clean under cold running water, removing all beards and dirt. Discard any mussels that don't close when you tap on them.

⊠ Add the mussels to the soup and cook for a couple of minutes. Carefully add the fish. Cover with a lid and cook on low heat until the mussels have opened. It takes about four minutes.

⊠ Add the shrimp and herbs, carefully, so the fish doesn't fall apart. Serve the soup with a dollop of orange aioli.

ORANGE AIOLI WITH A KICK

⊠ Make sure all ingredients are room temperature.

⊠ Whisk together garlic and egg yolks in a bowl, or use a food processor.

⊠ Add the oil, one drop at a time, while whisking. Be careful not to pour it in too quickly, or it won't blend properly.

⊠ Add orange zest, and season to taste with sambal oelek and salt. Let the flavors settle for at least an hour before serving. The aioli is also great for dipping the bread.

SCAMPI WITH CHILI AND GARLIC

4 servings

approx 24 raw, scaled tiger shrimp, or scampi
*   tails*
1 red chili
3 garlic cloves
2 tsp freshly grated ginger
1 tsp ground cumin
1 tsp paprika
4 tbsp olive oil
3 tbsp chopped cilantro
salt

serve with:
lemon wedges
good bread

This is a quick and easy dish that is perfect as an appetizer or starter.

⊠ Split the chili in two, remove the seeds and white veins, and slice finely. Chop the garlic.

⊠ Sauté the chili, garlic, ginger, cumin, and paprika in olive oil, without browning them.

⊠ Add the shrimp to the spice mix and fry for two to three minutes. The shrimp is done when they turn red. It's important not to overcook them, as they will be dry.

⊠ Add cilantro, and season to taste with salt.

MARINATED SQUID

4 servings

approx 3⅓ lbs (600 g) squid
lightly salted water for boiling

marinade:
1 red chili
2 garlic cloves
6 tbsp olive oil
2 tbsp freshly squeezed lemon juice
3 tbsp chopped parsley
2 tbsp chopped cilantro
½ tsp lemon zest
salt

There are many ways to serve different kinds of dishes. One way is to set up an in-home buffet. I also like to begin a meal with various mezze and quality bread. It's delicious and fun to prepare; there are so many different varieties! I make different mezze for every meal. Sometimes, I like to make this squid dish.

⊠ Start with the marinade: Split the chili in two, remove the seeds and white veins, and slice finely. Chop the garlic. Mix all the ingredients.

⊠ Prepare the squid: Remove the head. Use your fingers to remove the sticky insides, and the part that looks like a transparent piece of plastic. Tear the skin off, starting in the back where the fin is. Rinse the squid well, inside and out.

⊠ Bring lightly salted water to a boil. Cook the squid for about three minutes. It's important not to overcook it, as it will get rubbery. Drain, and cut the squid into thin circles.

⊠ Put the warm squid in the marinade and leave to marinate for at least two hours, preferably longer.

SPICY SARDINES WITH FENNEL SALAD

4 servings

1⅓ lbs (600 g) fillet of herring or sardines

marinade:
1 tsp cumin seeds
1 tsp coriander seeds
1 tbsp grated onion
2 garlic cloves, pressed
5 tbsp olive oil
2 tbsp freshly squeezed lemon juice
1 tsp paprika
a pinch of chili powder
2 tbsp chopped cilantro
1 tbsp chopped mint
salt

breading:
½ tsp salt
½ cup (100 ml) coarse rye flour
butter for frying

2 oranges
2 red grapefruits
1 fennel
1 small red onion
1 red chili
2 tbsp chopped cilantro
the juice from the citrus fruits
3 tbsp olive oil
salt and freshly grated pepper

In this corner of the world, people love sardines. For a Scandinavian version, I use herring, which is also really delicious. Serve it with potato purée or a salad with fennel and citrus fruits, or both.

⊠ Start with the marinade: Roast the cumin seeds in a dry pan. Crush them together with the coriander seeds using a mortar and pestle. Mix all the ingredients.

⊠ Rinse the fish fillets in water and pat them dry. Mix the fillets with the marinade and marinate for at least two hours, preferably longer.

⊠ If you're using an outdoor barbecue, it's easiest to cook the fillets in a grill basket over embers.

⊠ If you prefer to fry your fish, it's best to add some breading first. Cover the fillets in rye flour with salt, and fry them in butter.

FENNEL SALAD

⊠ Peel the oranges and the grapefruits with a knife, removing all the white pith. Cut it into segments, discarding the membranes. Save the juices from cutting the oranges for the dressing.

⊠ Inspect the fennel and slice it finely. Finely chop the onion. Split the chili in half and remove the seeds and the white veins.

⊠ Mix fruit and vegetables in a bowl. Dress with the juice from the citrus fruits and olive oil. Season to taste with salt and pepper. Let the salad marinate for at least an hour before serving.

FISH BURGERS WITH CUCUMBER YOGURT

6 servings

fish patties:
1⅓ lbs (600 g) cod fillet, fresh or thawed
1 red chili
½ packet (¼ g) saffron threads
½ tsp hot water
½ cup (100 ml) chopped parsley
2 eggs
1 tsp salt
butter for frying

cucumber yogurt:
¾ cup (200 ml) plain yogurt
⅔ cup (150 ml) cucumber, diced
2 tbsp chopped mint
½ tsp ground cumin
salt and freshly ground pepper

serve with:
cucumber yogurt
warm pita
shredded lettuce
sliced tomatoes
sliced red onion

Most people immediately associate burgers with ground beef. Sure, a hamburger will always be a hamburger. But there are so many variations: turkey burgers, fish burgers, vegetarian burgers. . . . I prefer fish. I make my burgers by stuffing pita bread with fish and cucumber yogurt.

◻ Start by mixing all the ingredients for the cucumber yogurt.

◻ Dice the fish finely. Split the chili in half, remove the seeds and the white veins, and chop the chili. Mix the saffron with the hot water.

◻ Mix all the ingredients for the patties.

◻ With wet hands, shape the mixture into six patties. Fry in butter until the patties are golden on both sides. They should be just cooked through. Don't cook them for too long, or they will become dry.

◻ Carefully heat the pita bread in the oven. Stuff each bread with a fish patty, cucumber yogurt, salad, tomato, and onion. Serve immediately.

TROUT WITH COUSCOUS AND ALMONDS

4 servings

4 gutted trout, approx ¾ lb (375 g) each
salt and freshly ground pepper
4 tbsp olive oil
½ cup (50 g) almond flakes
cooking twine

couscous:
2 shallots
2 garlic cloves
2 tbsp olive oil
½ cup (125 ml) water
½ vegetable bouillon cube
a dash of harissa, store bought
   or homemade (p. 27)
½ cup (125 ml) couscous
1 tsp lemon zest
3 tbsp chopped parsley
1 tbsp chopped mint

serve with:
lemon wedges

Trout with almonds is a French classic, and Moroccan cooking is very much influenced by French cuisine, as Morocco was once a French colony. Stuff the trout with lemony couscous, top it off with olive oil and sliced almonds, and bake it in the oven. Doesn't it sound delicious?

⊠ Start with the couscous: Finely chop the shallots and garlic. Heat olive oil in a pot, and sauté the shallots and garlic, without browning them. Add water, bouillon, and harissa, and bring to a boil.

⊠ Add the couscous, cover with a lid, and remove from the heat. Let the couscous swell for about five minutes. Use a fork to stir the couscous fluffy. Let it cool, then add lemon zest, parsley, and mint.

⊠ Preheat the oven to 400°F (200°C). Rinse the fish in cold water and pat dry. Add salt and pepper to the fish, inside and out. Stuff the trout with the couscous, and use twine to tie them shut. You may need a second pair of hands for this part, as it can be hard to keep the couscous from falling out. Place the fish in a large, greased oven proof dish or on a greased oven sheet. Mix olive oil and almonds, and spread over the fish. Cook in the middle of the oven until the almonds' color is right, and the fish is cooked through. It takes about twenty minutes.

MEDITERRANEAN FISH STEW

4 servings

1⅓ lbs (600 g) monkfish fillet
1 batch chermoula (p. 25)
1 red bell pepper
1 yellow bell pepper
approx 16 small new potatoes or other small
   potatoes
4 garlic cloves, chopped
4 tbsp olive oil
1⅓ cups (250 g) cherry tomatoes
½ cup (100 ml) black olives with pits, such
   as kalamata
salt and freshly ground pepper
½ cup (100 ml) water

serve with:
good bread

All-in-one stews are always practical. For this stew, I use monkfish, which has a firm texture and won't easily break apart. The fish is first marinated, then cooked with peppers, potatoes, tomatoes, and olives. Simply put, it's a Mediterranean fish stew.

▨ Start by making the spice mix "chermoula." Preheat the oven to 450°F (250°C). Remove the seeds from the peppers, and slice them coarsely. Grill them, high in the oven, until their skins are charred and blistered. It takes about fifteen minutes. Remove the skins. If it's hard to remove the skins, put the peppers in a plastic bag for about ten minutes and try again.

▨ Dice the fish and marinate it, using most of the chermoula. Let it sit for about an hour. Save a couple of tablespoons of the chermoula for later.

▨ Parboil the potatoes in lightly salted water for about ten minutes. Drain and split the potatoes in half.

▨ Sauté the garlic with two tablespoons of olive oil, without browning it. Add the tomatoes and cover with a lid. Cook over low heat until the tomatoes are soft. Crush them a bit using a wooden ladle. Add the peppers, olives, and the remaining chermoula. Season to taste with salt and pepper.

▨ Cover the bottom of a stew pot with the potatoes. Add about half of the tomato sauce, and then the fish with the marinade. Pour the rest of the tomato sauce and olive oil on top. Pour in the water.

▨ Cover with a lid and cook on low heat for about fifteen minutes, until the fish and potatoes are cooked through. Serve the stew with some quality bread.

COD QUENELLES IN TOMATO SAUCE

4 servings

quenelles:
1⅓ lbs (600 g) fillet of cod, or other
*   similar fish*
1 slice of day-old white bread
1 tsp salt
¼ cup (50 ml) plain yogurt
½ cup (100 ml) chopped parsley
3 tbsp chopped cilantro
a pinch of cayenne pepper
1 egg

tomato sauce:
2 shallots
2 garlic cloves
1 chili
olive oil
1 tsp paprika
½ tsp crushed coriander seeds
1 tsp ground cumin
28 oz (800 g) canned diced tomatoes
1 tbsp tomato purée
2 chicken bouillon cubes
¾ cup (200 ml) water
salt

garnish:
chopped parsley

In Scandinavia, where I'm from, children grow up eating canned fish balls. This is similar, but also completely different. In Morocco you make the fish balls from scratch, and cook them in a tasty tomato sauce.

The quenelles:
Cut the crusts off the bread and soak it in cold water for about ten minutes. Carefully squeeze the water out.

Cut the fish into smaller pieces and then shred it in a food processor. Blend together with salt. It should make a rough paste. Add the rest of the ingredients and mix to make a batter. Let it rest in the fridge for about an hour.

Shape the batter into balls. Cook half of the balls in the tomato sauce for about five minutes on one side, then turn them and cook for another five minutes. Remove from the sauce and repeat the process with the rest of the fish balls.

Put all fish balls into the sauce and heat carefully. Top with chopped parsley.

The tomato sauce:
Chop the shallots and garlic. Split the chili in half, remove the seeds and white veins, and chop finely.

Add olive oil to a large pan and sauté the shallots and garlic for a few minutes, without browning them. Add the chili and the spices when it's almost done. Add tomatoes, tomato purée, bouillon, and water. Let the sauce simmer over low heat, with the lid ajar, until the sauce has thickened. It takes about twenty minute. Season to taste with salt.

STUFFED GRAPE LEAVES WITH SWEET AND SOUR SAUCE

4–6 servings

1–1⅓ lbs (500–600 g) fillet of fish with
    firm flesh, such as tuna, monkfish,
    or swordfish
approx 30 grape leaves
olive oil
cocktail toothpicks

marinade:
2 tbsp chopped cilantro
2 garlic cloves, pressed
1 tsp ground cumin
4 tbsp olive oil
3 tbsp freshly squeezed lemon juice
salt

sauce:
1 small shallot
2 garlic cloves
½ red chili
½ packet (¼ g) saffron threads
1 tbsp hot water
4 tbsp freshly squeezed lemon juice
4 tbsp powdered sugar
1 tbsp chopped cilantro
1 tbsp chopped mint

Perhaps you've visited Greece and tried stuffed grape leaves with bread and tzatziki. If so, you won't find this dish all that unusual. I often visit ethnic markets because of their exciting range of products and good prices. The shop staff is always helpful, and answers all of my questions no matter how stupid they may be. That's how I discovered grape leaves. They are preserved in brine, and you can find them either canned or in bulk. These are perfect as a snack, as a starter, or on the buffet table. Serve them with a sweet and sour saffron sauce.

The fish:

⊠ Mix all the ingredients for the marinade. Dice the fish (you want cubes about 1" by 1" in size). Marinate for one to two hours.

⊠ Parboil the grape leaves in boiling water for about five minutes. Drain through a colander and leave to dry on a paper towel. Preheat the oven to 425°F (225°C).

⊠ Put a piece of fish on each grape leaf. If the leaves are small, use two. Fold the leaves to make little bundles. Place them, with the edges facing down, on an oven sheet lined with parchment paper. Brush with a little bit of olive oil.

⊠ Cook the fish packages high in the oven for about five minutes. It's important not to overcook the fish, as that will make it dry. Stick a cocktail toothpick in each bundle and dip them in the sauce.

The sauce:

⊠ Finely chop the shallots and garlic. Split the chili in half, remove the seeds and white veins, and chop finely. Mix the saffron with the hot water.

⊠ Mix all ingredients for the sauce and let the flavors settle for at least an hour before serving. Pour the sauce into several little bowls, so that each guest gets their own.

GRILLED SCAMPI SKEWERS

4 skewers

20 raw, peeled tiger shrimp or scampi tails
4 skewers
salt

marinade:
1 red chili
3 tbsp olive oil
2 tbsp freshly squeezed lemon juice
1 tsp ground cumin
2 garlic cloves, pressed
2 tbsp chopped mint
2 tbsp chopped cilantro

serve with:
lemon wedges
salad

Why make things difficult when something this simple can be so tasty? Serve with lemon wedges and a delicious salad.

▣ Split the chili in half, remove the seeds and white veins, and chop finely. Mix all the ingredients for the marinade.

▣ Put your shrimp in a bowl, add the marinade, and mix well. Marinate for at least an hour.

▣ If you are using wooden skewers, soak them in cold water for a while so they won't burn easily. Preheat the oven to 450°F (250°C), using the grill setting, or fire up the barbecue.

▣ Thread the shrimp on the skewers. Cook high in the oven, or on the barbecue, for about five minutes. Turn them once. Add salt.

GRILLED FISH SKEWERS

4 servings

1⅓ lbs (600 g) fillet of fish with firm
*   flesh, such as swordfish, tuna, monkfish,*
*   halibut, or salmon*
4 skewers
salt

marinade:
2 tbsp olive oil
4 tbsp chopped parsley
2 cloves of garlic, pressed
2 tsp ground cumin
1½ tsp ground ginger
2 tsp paprika
½ tsp chili powder

serve with:
lime or lemon wedges

When barbecuing fish, use fish with firm flesh that won't break apart easily.

▣ Mix the ingredients for the marinade. Dice the fish. Pat the marinade all over the fish and let it sit for one to two hours.

▣ If you are using wooden skewers, soak them in cold water for a while so they won't burn easily. Preheat the oven to 450°F (250°C), using the grill setting, or fire up the barbecue.

▣ Thread the fish cubes on the skewers. Place them on a greased oven sheet and cook high in the oven, or on the barbecue, for about five minutes. Turn them once.

▣ It is important not to overcook the fish, as that will make it dry. Remove the skewers from the heat just before the fish is done. Add salt.

BREAD, BAKED GOODS
& DESSERTS

SESAME RINGS

16 pieces

⅓ cup (75 ml) sesame seeds
½ oz (12½ g) active dry yeast
1⅓ cups (300 ml) water
1 tsp salt
3 tbsp olive oil
approx 3 cups (700 ml) all-purpose flour

top with:
1 egg
sesame seeds

Roasting the sesame seeds gives them so much more flavor, so don't skip that part.

▨ Toast the sesame seeds in an ungreased pan.

▨ Crumble the yeast in a bowl. Heat the water until it's warm: 100°F (37°C). Mix the yeast with the water. Add salt, olive oil, sesame seeds, and the flour, pouring only a little bit at a time. Mix until you have a smooth dough. Cover the bowl with a towel and leave it to rise for about half an hour.

▨ Sprinkle flour over the table or counter top where you want to work your dough. Knead the dough. Split it into sixteen pieces and shape into 8-inch ropes. Twist the ropes a few times, and then pinch the ends together to make rings.

▨ Place the rings on an oven sheet lined with parchment paper. Cover them with a towel and leave them to rise for about twenty minutes. Preheat the oven to 425°F (225°C).

▨ Beat the egg. Brush the rings with egg and sprinkle sesame seeds on top. Bake in the middle of the oven for twelve to fifteen minutes. Let them cool under a towel.

▨ Serve the sesame rings immediately, or keep them in the freezer and heat them carefully when you want to eat them.

SPICY BREAD CAKES

12 pieces

½ oz (12½ g) active dry yeast
    2 cups (500 ml) water
1 tsp salt
3 tbsp olive oil
1 tsp honey
1¾ cups (400 ml) durum wheat flour
3–3⅓ cups (700–800 ml) bread flour, such
    as whole wheat, rye, and/or barley

top with:
olive oil
paprika
sesame seeds
sea salt

Flatbread cakes, brushed with olive oil and sprinkled with different spice blends, are common in Morocco. They are quite similar to the Italian focaccia. You could call this a primitive sort of pizza, since pizza was originally plain old flatbread that gradually evolved as toppings were added. Bread, like other food, traveled across the Mediterranean.

▨ Crumble the yeast in a bowl. Heat the water until it's warm: 99°F (37°C). Mix the yeast with the water. Add salt, olive oil, honey, and flour, pouring a little bit at a time. Mix until you have a smooth dough. Cover the bowl with a towel and leave it to rise for about half an hour.

▨ Sprinkle flour over the table or counter top where you want to work your dough. Knead the dough. Split it into twelve pieces, shape them into balls, and use a rolling pin to make round cakes, about six inches wide.

▨ Place the breads on an oven sheet lined with parchment paper. Cover them with a towel and leave them to rise for about twenty minutes. Preheat the oven to 425°F (225°C).

▨ Brush with olive oil. Use a tea strainer to sprinkle the paprika evenly over the bread. Top with sesame seeds and a bit of sea salt. Bake in the middle of the oven for ten to twelve minutes. Let the bread cool a little before serving it, fresh out of the oven.

ANISE BREAD

6 pieces

¾ oz (25 g) active dry yeast
2 cups (500 ml) water
1½ tsp salt
3 tbsp olive oil
1 tsp honey
3 tbsp crushed anise seeds
approx 2 cups (500 ml) bread flour, such as
    whole wheat, rye, and/or barley
3–3½ cups (700–800 ml) all-purpose flour

top with:
water
anise seeds

Bread is an essential part of Moroccan cuisine. Moroccans tend to use bread in place of plates. It is always fresh, since house-wives bake every day. Few people have their own ovens, which is why it's a sight in Morocco to see women and children carrying baking sheets and baskets with fresh or uncooked bread on their heads. They are on their way to and from the wood burning ovens at the public baking houses. They're a clever invention, I must say. The store-bought bread I'm used to is nothing compared to what comes out of the baking houses.

▨ Crumble the yeast in a bowl. Heat the water until it's warm: 99°F (37°C). Mix the yeast with the water. Add salt, olive oil, honey, anise seeds, and flour, pouring a little bit at a time. Mix until you have a smooth dough. Cover the bowl with a towel and leave it to rise for about half an hour.

▨ Sprinkle flour over the table or counter top where you want to work your dough. Knead the dough. Split it into six pieces, shape them into balls, and use a rolling pin to make circles about one finger thick, and roughly seven inches wide.

▨ Use a sharp knife to cut an X in the middle of each bread, halfway through. Cover them with a towel and leave to rise for about twenty minutes. Preheat the oven to 400°F (200°C).

▨ Brush with water and sprinkle with anise seeds. Bake in the middle of the oven until the breads have the desired color. It takes about twenty minutes. Let them cool under a towel.

▨ Serve immediately, or keep them in the freezer and heat them carefully when you want to eat them.

ORIENTAL ONION BREAD

30 loaves

dough:
¾ oz (25 g) active dry yeast
approx 2 cups (500 ml) water
2 tsp salt
3 tbsp olive oil
1 tbsp honey
approx 6 cups (1¼ liters) all-purpose flour

filling:
3½ tbsp (50 g) butter, room temperature
1 shallot, chopped
2 garlic cloves, pressed
½ cup (100 ml) parsley, chopped
½ tsp ground cumin
½ tsp paprika
a pinch of chili powder

Portion sized loaves filled with oriental spiced butter.

▣ Mix the ingredients for the filling.

▣ Crumble the yeast in a bowl. Heat the water until it's warm: 99°F (37°C). Mix the yeast with the water. Add salt, olive oil, honey, and flour, a little bit at a time. Mix until you have a smooth dough. Cover the bowl with a towel and leave it to rise for about half an hour.

▣ Sprinkle flour over the table or counter top where you want to work your dough. Split it in two. Use a rolling pin to make thin squares. Spread the filling on top and roll up like a Swiss roll. Cut the rolls at an angle to make about thirty triangular pieces about an inch to an inch and a half wide.

▣ Place the breads on oven sheets lined with parchment paper, and sprinkle some flour over them. Cover with a towel and leave to rise for about twenty minutes. Preheat the oven to 425°F (225°C).

▣ Bake in the middle of the oven for ten to twelve minutes. Let them cool under a towel.

▣ Serve immediately, or keep them in the freezer and heat them carefully when you want to eat them.

GAZELLE HORNS

10 pieces

1 package frozen pre-rolled puff pastry,
*   approx 17 oz (425 g)*
¾–1 lb (400–500 g) almond paste, or
*   marzipan*
1 tbsp butter, room temperature
approx ½ cup (100 ml) powdered sugar,
*   sifted*
1½ tsp cinnamon
1 tsp orange flower water, or a little bit of
*   grated orange zest*

top with:
1 egg, beaten
sesame seeds
orange flower water
powdered sugar

Almond filled puff pastry with cinnamon and orange flower water. These horn-shaped pastries are widely popular, and are often called the national pastry of Morocco. I like to serve these as dessert with a fresh fruit salad and a dollop of crème fraîche or sour cream.

⊠ Follow the instructions on the package to thaw the puff pastry. Preheat the oven to 400°F (200°C).

⊠ Grate the almond paste or marzipan roughly. Mix with butter, powdered sugar, and cinnamon. Add orange flower water or orange zest.

⊠ Shape into bent "horns"—thick on one end and thin on the other.

⊠ Split the puff pastry and roll out slightly with a rolling pin. Twist pastry around the marzipan horns. Cut off any excess pastry, and pinch together well. Place the pastries on a baking sheet lined with parchment paper.

⊠ Brush the horns with beaten egg and sprinkle with sesame seeds. Bake in the middle of the oven until the puff pastry is crisp and golden. It takes about twelve to fifteen minutes.

⊠ Let the pastries cool, lightly brush with some orange flower water (optional) and sift powdered sugar on top.

DATE COOKIES

approx 40 cookies

9 oz (250 g) dried dates
½ cup (100 ml) water
1⅔ cups (400 ml) all-purpose flour
¼ cup (50 ml) sugar
½ cup (125 g) butter, cold
2–3 tbsp cold water
approx 1 tsp orange flower water, or a little
*   bit of orange zest*

top with:
powdered sugar

Dried fruit is a must during the holidays, and I always make these cookies for Christmas. But who is to say when cookies are in season? Date cookies are delicious any time of the year.

⊠ Remove the seeds from the dates, and chop them coarsely. Bring the water to a boil, cover with a lid and cook the dates over low heat for five to seven minutes, until they are soft. Drain, but save the water.

⊠ Sift the flour into the bowl of a food processor. Add the sugar and the butter, cut into pieces. Mix to make a rough paste. Add two to three tablespoons of the (now cold) water, and the dates, and mix for a few seconds.

⊠ Pour the batter into a bowl, add the orange flower water, and kneed to make a dough. Cover with plastic wrap and let it rest in the fridge for about an hour.

⊠ Preheat the oven to 400°F (200°C). Use a teaspoon to measure equally sized cookies. Shape them into balls, and place on oven sheets lined with parchment paper. Flatten each cookie a little. Bake in the middle of the oven for about fifteen minutes. Sift powdered sugar on top.

APRICOTS IN PHYLLO

10 pieces

1 package frozen pre-rolled phyllo, approx
  16 oz (425 g)
10 canned apricot halves
5⅓ oz (150 g) almond paste, or marzipan
1 lemon, zest
½ tsp cinnamon
1 tbsp chopped mint
a few drops of orange flower water

top with:
1 egg, beaten
powdered sugar

serve with:
lightly whipped cream

Phyllo pastries with apricots and marzipan. Sounds heavenly, doesn't it? Thanks to frozen phyllo, everyone can be a pastry chef. Whipping up delicious and delicate pastries becomes so easy. Serve these straight from the oven, with a dollop of lightly whipped cream.

⌧ Preheat the oven to 425°F (225°C). Follow the instructions on the package to thaw the phyllo. Drain the apricots.

⌧ Grate the almond paste or marzipan finely. Mix with lemon, cinnamon, mint, and orange flower water (optional).

⌧ Cut the phyllo sheets and roll out to five-inch squares.

⌧ Put half an apricot on each sheet, with the round side down. Divide the marzipan mix on top of the apricots and squeeze it together to make a ball.

⌧ Fold the dough to make a triangle package, and use a fork to pinch the edges together. Place the pastries on an oven sheet lined with parchment paper, and brush with a beaten egg.

⌧ Bake in the middle of the oven for twelve to fifteen minutes, until the pastry is crisp and golden. Let them cool a little, then sift powdered sugar on top and serve with a dollop of lightly whipped cream.

SPICY SAFFRON PEARS

6 servings

6 average sized, firm pears
1 vanilla bean or 1 tsp vanilla extract
1 packet (½ g) saffron threads
1 cinnamon stick
2 cloves
6 tbsp honey
approx 3½ tbsp (50 ml) tbsp freshly
  squeezed lemon juice
approx 1⅔ cups (400 ml) water

serve with:
vanilla ice cream

Poached fruit is the perfect dessert for fall and winter. Honey, saffron, cinnamon, and cloves give these golden pears an exciting, spiced flavor. If you have any syrup left over, save it and serve with vanilla ice cream, or add canned pears and heat it up again.

▨ Peel the pears, but leave the stem.

▨ Split the vanilla bean in half, and scrape the seeds into a large pan. Add the bean halves (or the vanilla extract), spices, honey, lemon, and water into a large pan.

▨ Bring to a boil and add the pears. Cover with a lid and cook until the pears have softened slightly. Turn them a few times. The cooking time depends on the size of the pears; twenty to forty minutes. Use a fork to see when they're ready.

▨ Let the pears cool in the syrup, spooning the syrup over them a few times. Serve warm with some of the syrup and vanilla ice cream.

APPLE WEDGES WITH ROSE WATER AND CINNAMON

6 apples
3½ tbsp (50 g) butter
1 tsp ground cinnamon
3 tbsp honey
1 tbsp freshly squeezed lemon juice
1 tbsp rose water

serve with:
vanilla ice cream

Apple wedges, sautéed with honey, cinnamon, and a splash of rose water. I'd call this a Swedish/Moroccan crossover. Serve the apple wedges warm, with some vanilla ice cream.

▨ Peel the apples, cut them in wedges, and remove the cores.

▨ Melt the butter in a large pan. Sauté the apples on all sides for a few minutes, then add cinnamon, honey, lemon juice, and rose water. Let it simmer for a minute or so, until the syrup has thickened and the apples have just softened.

▨ Serve immediately with vanilla ice cream.

PISTACHIO PARFAIT

8 servings

2⅓ oz (150 g) peeled pistachios, unsalted
4 egg yolks
½ cup (100 ml) powdered sugar
4 egg whites + 4 tbsp sugar
approx 1⅔ cups (400 ml) whipping cream
a few drops of green food coloring
2 tbsp rose water (optional)

serve with:
raspberries or strawberries

I keep reading all these tempting recipes for ice cream, but I can't make any of them because I, like most people, don't own an ice cream maker! Luckily for me, it's completely possible to make a smooth, creamy parfait without any special equipment. This one has an interesting flavor: pistachio and rose water. If you can't find any rose water, it's delicious without it as well.

⊠ Grind the nuts finely in a food processor. Beat the egg yolks with the powdered sugar until fluffy. Beat egg whites and granulated sugar to a firm meringue foam. Whip the cream.

⊠ Mix the pistachios with the egg yolk batter. Add food coloring and rose water (optional). Add the whipped cream. Finally, fold in the egg whites.

⊠ Pour the batter into a container that can hold about a half gallon. I usually cover the container in plastic wrap first. This makes it easier to remove the parfait when it's done, and avoids the mess that can come with having to rinse the container under hot water. Cover with a lid or plastic wrap, and freeze for at least four hours.

⊠ Remove the parfait from the freezer before serving. Turn the container over onto a pretty serving dish.

ORANGE SALAD WITH CINNAMON

4 servings

4 oranges
2 tsp powdered sugar
1 tsp cinnamon
approx ½ cup (100 ml) shredded dates

top with:
fresh mint

This is Morocco's number one dessert. They serve it everywhere. It's fresh and easy to make.

⊠ Peel the oranges with a sharp knife, removing all the white pith. Cut into thin slices, across the membranes.

⊠ Spread the orange slices over a nice dish, overlapping a bit. Sift powdered sugar and cinnamon over the oranges. You can use a tea strainer for this part. Top with the dates, cover with plastic wrap, and let the salad rest in the fridge for about an hour before serving.

⊠ Decorate with fresh mint.

FRUIT SALAD WITH POMEGRANATE AND DATES

4 servings

2 pomegranates
4 oranges
1 red grapefruit
6 fresh dates
2 tbsp chopped mint
1 tbsp honey

serve with:
Greek yogurt

Mmm . . . Fruit salad with pomegranate, citrus fruits, dates, honey, and mint. Can a dessert get any fresher? The countries around the Mediterranean make delicious yogurt, which used to be hard to get a hold of around the rest of the world. Now we can find Greek yogurt at most supermarkets.

⊠ Split the pomegranates and scoop the seeds out into a bowl, using the handle of a spoon. Remove the white pith, which is bitter.

⊠ Peel the oranges and grapefruit with a sharp knife, removing all the white pith. Cut into segments and discard the membranes. Remove the seeds from the dates and chop finely.

⊠ Mix all the ingredients and let the flavors blend in the fridge for about an hour. Serve with a dollop of Greek yogurt.

COUSCOUS FOR DESSERT

4 servings

1 cup (250 ml) couscous
1 cup (250 ml) water
6 dried dates
3–4 dried figs

syrup:
¾ cup (200 ml) water
3 tbsp honey
1 tsp ground cinnamon

top with:
3½ tbsp blanched almonds
3½ tbsp walnuts
cinnamon
orange flower water (optional)

serve with:
Greek yogurt

Couscous for dessert might sound a bit strange, but there are numerous desserts everywhere in the world with a grain base.

▨ Put the couscous grains in a bowl. Bring the water to a boil and pour over the couscous. Cover with aluminum foil and let the couscous swell for about five minutes. Stir with a fork to make it fluffy.

▨ Remove the seeds from the dates and chop finely.

▨ Bring water and honey to a boil, and let it simmer over low heat for about five minutes, until it has thickened. Season with cinnamon. Add the dried fruit to the syrup and let it simmer for another few minutes.

▨ Pour the the fruit syrup over the warm couscous and mix well. Let it cool.

▨ Top with roughly chopped almonds, walnuts, and a little cinnamon. Splash some orange flower water over it if you like, and serve with Greek yogurt.

INDEX

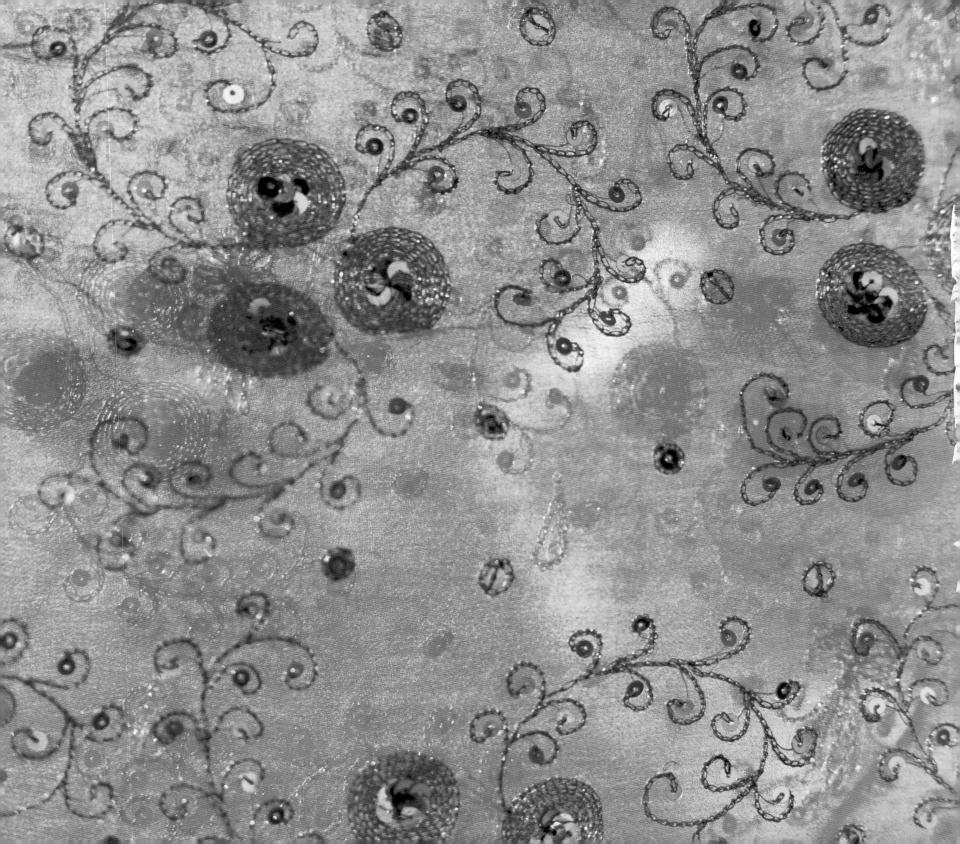